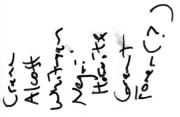

A House Divided

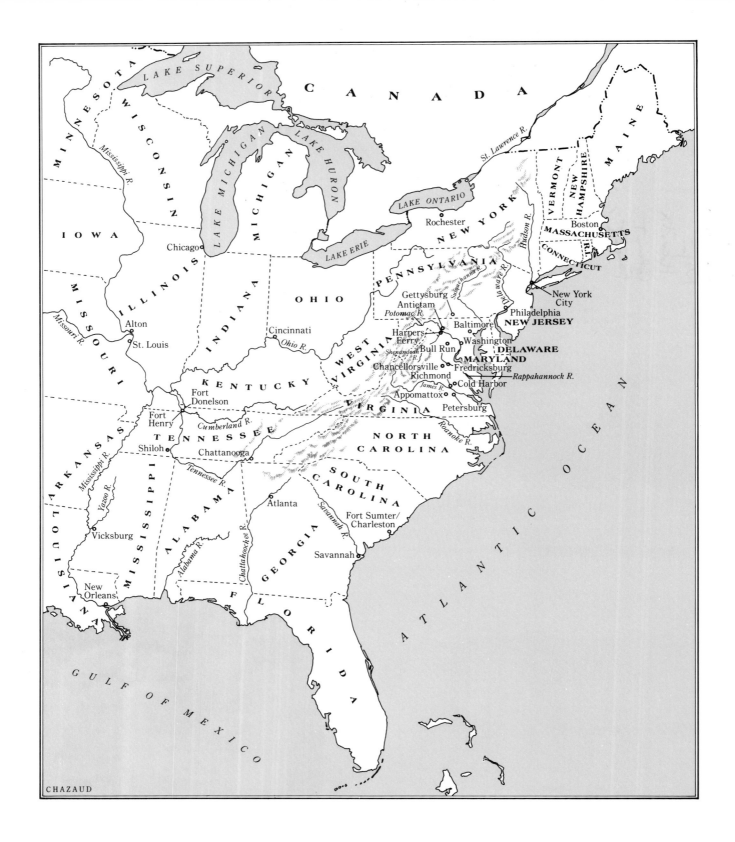

CHAZAUD

A HOUSE DIVIDED

America in the Age of Lincoln

ERIC FONER

OLIVIA MAHONEY

CHICAGO HISTORICAL SOCIETY
IN ASSOCIATION WITH
W. W. NORTON & COMPANY
NEW YORK   LONDON

The text of this book is composed in Bulmer, with display type set in Biltmore, Bulmer, and Engravers Bold. Composition by PennSet, Inc. Manufacturing by The Murray Printing Company. Book design by Charlotte Staub.

First published as a Norton paperback 1991

Library of Congress Cataloging-in-Publication Data

Foner, Eric.
    A house divided : America in the age of Lincoln / I. Eric Foner.—1st ed. II. Olivia Mahoney
        p.   cm.
    Catalog of an exhibition held at the Chicago Historical Society.
    1. United States—History—1849–1877—Exhibitions. 2. United States—History—Civil War, 1861—1865—Exhibitions. 3. Lincoln, Abraham, 1809–1865—Exhibitions. 4. Chicago Historical Society—Exhibitions. I. Chicago Historical Society. II. Title.
E415.7.F66 1990
973.7′074′77311—dc20   89-9239

ISBN 0-393-30612-7

W. W. Norton & Company, Inc., 500 Fifth Avenue, New York, N.Y. 10110
W. W. Norton & Company Ltd, 10 Coptic Street, London WC1A 1PU

2 3 4 5 6 7 8 9 0

TO

Jack and Liza Foner

AND

Miriam, Ellen, and Anne Bouleanu

THE CHICAGO HISTORICAL SOCIETY'S EXHIBITION
A HOUSE DIVIDED: AMERICA IN THE AGE OF LINCOLN
WOULD NOT HAVE BEEN POSSIBLE WITHOUT
THE EXTRAORDINARY GENEROSITY OF:

Kraft General Foods
National Endowment for the Humanities, a federal agency

MAJOR SUPPORT ALSO HAS COME FROM THE FOLLOWING:

Blum-Kovler Foundation
Amoco Foundation
The Regenstein Foundation
Sears, Roebuck and Co.
The Guild of the Chicago Historical Society
Crate & Barrel
Illinois Humanities Council
The Joyce Foundation
The Leo Burnett Company, Inc.
Illinois Department of Commerce and Community Affairs/Office of Tourism

AND ADDITIONAL GIFTS HAVE BEEN RECEIVED FROM:

Fuji Photo Film U.S.A., Inc.
Mr. and Mrs. Benjamin Gingiss
Helen M. Harrison Foundation
IMC Foundation
Mr. and Mrs. Richard M. Jaffee
Mr. and Mrs. Thomas L. Jones
Mr. and Mrs. James Kackley
Mr. and Mrs. W. Paul Krauss
The Nalco Foundation
Polk Bros. Foundation
Underwriters Laboratories, Inc.

CONTENTS

PREFACE

A century and a quarter after its conclusion, the Civil War remains a subject of fascination for Americans. For the war, the greatest crisis in our history, raised the decisive questions of America's national existence—the relations between local and national government, the balance between force and consent in generating obedience to authority, the definition of citizenship, the meaning of liberty and equality. For those who lived through it, the Civil War would always remain the central event of their lives. In the physical destruction and economic changes it wrought, as in its introduction of new ideas and diffusion of enduring sectional passions, the war altered the lives and consciousness of several generations of Americans, and its most important consequences—the preservation of the Union and the destruction of slavery—permanently affected the future course of national development.

At the root of the crisis that produced the Civil War lay slavery, the "peculiar institution" of the Old South. During the first half of the nineteenth century, the Union created by the Declaration of Independence and the Constitution became divided into slave and free regions, each following a distinct course of economic, social, and intellectual development. The existence of slavery in the Southern states and its extension into the Western territories became the focus of an acrimonious national debate that divided the churches, shattered the political parties, and helped bring on a military confrontation in which over 600,000 Americans perished. Begun to preserve the Union in the aftermath of the South's secession, the war became a struggle for emancipation that eradicated slavery from American society, but left to future generations the issue of racial justice.

A House Divided: America in the Age of Lincoln, is published in conjunction with a major exhibition on the Civil War era at the Chicago Historical Society.

Including some six hundred artifacts and images from the Society's vast collections, the exhibition examines the institution of slavery, explores the economic development of the antebellum North and West, traces the rise of the antislavery movement and the sectional political controversies that led to war, and treats the Civil War both as a bloody military confrontation and as a catalyst of far-reaching changes in American life. The exhibition features many of the individuals who shaped the era's history, from Frederick Douglass, who escaped from slavery to become an internationally renowned spokesman for the abolitionist cause, to Ulysses S. Grant, the principal architect of the Union's military victory. Most prominent of all, of course, is Abraham Lincoln, who appears at numerous points in the exhibition, not as a larger-than-life icon or unblemished hero, but as a man whose life (1809–1865) coincided with the emergence and resolution of the sectional controversy and whose career both reflected and helped to shape many of the significant developments in mid-nineteenth-century Northern life. Those who encounter the material culture of the past by visiting the exhibition will share an intellectual and emotional experience; for them, we hope this book prolongs and deepens that experience. For other readers, the book stands independently as a narrative of the Civil War era, illustrated by well over one hundred of the exhibition's most striking visual images.

In emphasizing how critical the slavery issue was to the origins and course of the Civil War, *A House Divided* reflects the thinking of the most recent generation of American historians. As Lincoln observed in his second inaugural address, everyone who lived through that era understood that slavery was "somehow" the cause of the war. This insight was abandoned by many historians earlier in this century, in favor of an emphasis on the tariff or other narrow economic questions as the root of the sectional crisis. Many scholars of an earlier generation viewed the war as a needless conflict between two fundamentally similar societies that went to war because irresponsible agitators inflamed public opinion and a "blundering generation" of political leaders proved unable to resolve the resulting crisis. In the past thirty years, however, thanks to an outpouring of scholarly studies on the peculiar institution and its impact on American life, historians are once again aware of the centrality of slavery to the course of nineteenth-century American history and of the fundamental divisions its presence created. This is not to suggest that the slavery controversy affected every American in the same way, or that issues like immigration and the tariff were not divisive. It simply means that it increasingly became impossible to think seriously about American society without somehow coming to grips with slavery, emancipation, and the Union. These are the themes that underlie the account of the Civil War era in *A House Divided*.

The exhibition on which this book is based resulted from the collaboration of an academic historian, Eric Foner of Columbia University, with the staff of the Chicago Historical Society. Committed to making the most current scholarship on historical subjects accessible to a wide public, the Society is increasingly turning to academic historians to work with its curators to develop exhibitions and interpret its collections. *We the People, 1765–1820*, a highly successful exhibition on the era of the American Revolution mounted by the Society in 1987, for which Alfred Young of Northern Illinois University served as guest curator, was the first of these collaborations.

The Society's Civil War–era collections are far more extensive than those for the revolutionary period, and the first task of the curators of *A House Divided* was to select exhibition items from the countless nineteenth-century paintings, prints, photographs, manuscripts, newspapers, books, maps, costumes, and other materials in the Society's holdings. For nearly a century, the Chicago Historical Society, through purchases and donations, has been collecting Civil War–era artifacts. The core of the collection was acquired in 1920 from Charles F. Gunther, Chicago candy manufacturer, city alderman, and collector *extraordinaire*, who had begun to amass Civil War materials and other pieces of Americana in the 1870s. In 1889, he used the bricks of Libby Prison (where captured Union soldiers had been incarcerated in Civil War Richmond) to construct a museum in Chicago to house his collection. When Gunther died in 1920, the Society purchased his holdings, which include many of the most important objects presented in the exhibition and reproduced in this book.

Every museum exhibition is a collaborative endeavor, and many people at the Chicago Historical Society deserve thanks for their contribution to this project. Ellsworth Brown, the Society's president and director, offered enthusiastic support and encouragement for the project from its initial stages. Susan Page Tillett coordinated and oversaw every phase as project director; her leadership and her high standards were critical to realizing the exhibition. Mary Janzen wrote successful planning and implementation grant proposals and gave valuable advice during the early planning stages. We are especially grateful to the National Endowment for the Humanities for their generous support enabling the curators to survey the collections and develop and implement the exhibition proposal. Marc Hilton, Barbara Reed, and other members of the Development staff raised additional funds for the project.

Andrew Leo's exhibition design, incorporating Bill Van Nimwegen's graphic work, brought artifacts and ideas together in engaging and imaginative ways. His sensitivity to the history of the period and the needs of the museum visitor is evident throughout the exhibition plan. Russell Lewis arranged the copublishing of this book. He edited the exhibition labels, with assistance from Aleta Zak and Claudia Coffee, and ensured that their intellectual interpretations be both rigorous and accessible. Amina Dickerson brought her wide-ranging experience with museum education to the project and was responsible for developing innovative and challenging programming to accompany the exhibition. Special thanks go to Virginia Heaven, who kept track of artifacts while in storage and while they were being photographed, conserved, and installed. She managed the day-to-day tasks of mounting the exhibition with exceptional efficiency and good humor. John Alderson, assisted by Jay Crawford, photographed the artifacts for publication. Thomas Skwerski proved a valuable research assistant during many critical phases of the exhibition's development. Sylvia Landsman typed drafts of illustration captions and the checklist for the book as well as the exhibition labels. Conservation of the artifacts was a monumental task carried out by a team of expert professionals: Anna Kolata worked on costumes, Carol Turchan on paper materials, and Jeanne Mandel, assisted by Colleen Tracy, Eileen Lynch, and Joseph T. Scott, on other three-dimensional objects.

A House Divided drew from nearly every collection at the Chicago Historical Society, and we are indebted to curatorial staff who assisted us in countless ways. We would especially like to thank the members of the Society's Civil War Committee, who originally undertook the challenge of organizing a new exhibition on Lincoln and the Civil War: Janice McNeill, Mary Janzen, Linda Evans, Elizabeth Jachimowicz, Carole Krucoff, and Joseph Zywicki. Other members of the curatorial staff—Archie Motley, Ralph Pugh, Larry Viskochil, Susan Samek, Maureen Will, Wendy Greenhouse, Clarence Clark, and Robert Goler—offered assistance, encouragement, and valuable advice. The project is also indebted to the volunteer efforts of Gary Snyderman, Paul Adler, and especially Patricia Lommel, who spent countless hours checking files, photocopying, and recording essential information.

Several distinguished scholars served as consultants for the exhibition, and their comments proved invaluable: Barbara J. Fields of Columbia University, Neil Harris of the University of Chicago, Leon F. Litwack of the University of California, Berkeley, Mark Neely of The Louis A. Warren Lincoln Library and Museum, Richard N. Current of the University of Wisconsin, John Simon of the Ulysses S. Grant Association, Charles B. Strozier of the John Jay College of Criminal Justice, Donald Kloster of the National Museum of American History, and Craddock Goins, curator emeritus of the Smithsonian Institution. Richard H. Sewell of the University of Wisconsin read the book manuscript and made numerous helpful suggestions. And Steven Forman of W. W. Norton & Company was an exceptionally efficient and understanding editor. Finally, we would like to thank our families for their encouragement and support throughout the challenging, arduous, but always fascinating process of turning 600 artifacts into a story—told through exhibition and book—of the most turbulent era in our nation's past.

Exhibition Curators
Eric Foner, Columbia University
Olivia Mahoney, Chicago Historical Society
May 1989

A House Divided

Cotton Pressing in Louisiana *from* Ballou's Magazine *in 1856, illustrates how slaves were used to supply power for a partially mechanized work process.*

ONE

THE PECULIAR

INSTITUTION

Nineteenth-century Americans inherited a divided legacy from the nation's founders. Liberty and slavery, democracy and despotism—these contradictions survived the revolutionary era and grew ever more glaring in the decades that followed. Even as slavery mocked America's professed ideals, slave labor played a critical role in the nation's growth, expanding westward with the young republic, producing the cotton that fueled the early industrial revolution. At the same time, however, the rapid expansion of the slave system in the first half of the nineteenth century divided the nation into two regions with fundamentally different economies, social structures, and values. Between them conflict was all but inevitable.

When Thomas Jefferson in 1776 proclaimed mankind's inalienable right to life, liberty, and the pursuit of happiness, slavery was already an old institution in America. For well over a century slaves had tilled the tobacco fields of Virginia and Maryland; for nearly as long they had labored on the rice plantations of coastal South Carolina. Slaves also worked on small farms in parts of the North, and in many artisan shops in cities like New York and Philadelphia. But since slavery was peripheral to the Northern economy, the number of slaves there remained tiny compared with the South. In 1776 slaves composed forty percent of the population of the colonies from Maryland south to Georgia, but well below ten percent in colonies to the north. Taking the nation as a whole, one American in five was a black slave when the war for independence began.

During the Revolution, slavery for the first time became the subject of intense public scrutiny. And the turmoil produced by the war, the implacable logic of revolutionary ideals, and the actions of blacks themselves all threatened to undermine the institution. With the British offering freedom to slaves who joined the royal cause, tens of thousands fled their owners and gained their liberty. Thousands of others escaped bondage by enlisting in the Revolutionary Army. During the 1780s a considerable number of slaveholders, especially in Virginia and Maryland, voluntarily emancipated their slaves, often citing the Revolution's principle of individual liberty as their reason. Many others hoped and believed that the institution would soon die out. "Nothing is more certainly written in the book of fate," wrote Jefferson, "than that these people are to be free." Unfortunately, like many others, the author of the Declaration of Independence failed to liberate his own slaves.

Throughout the nation, the manumissions of the revolutionary era created the first large free black communities, which rapidly constructed their own schools, churches, fraternal societies, Masonic lodges, and other institutions and searched for ways to assist their fellows in bondage. By 1790 nearly 60,000 free blacks lived in the United States; twenty years later their numbers had almost doubled, and they represented over one-tenth of the black population.

Among both blacks and whites, the Revolution inspired widespread hopes that slavery might be removed from American life. By the early nineteenth century every state from Pennsylvania north to New Hampshire had taken steps to abolish slavery, either by court decision, constitutional provision, or laws providing for gradual emancipation. Nonetheless the stark fact is that, despite manumission, the large number of blacks who escaped to freedom, and the

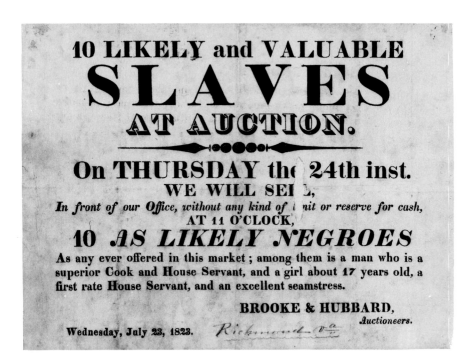

Slave sale broadside from Richmond, Virginia.

beginning of abolition in the North, there were more slaves at the end of the revolutionary era than at the beginning. The first national census, in 1790, reported that the half-million slave population of 1776 had grown to some 700,000, the vast majority living in the South. Paralyzed by the conviction that the two races could not live together on a basis of equality, and recognizing that abolition would produce severe economic dislocation, the Southern states resisted all talk of general emancipation. In 1806 Virginia acted to curtail voluntary manumission and the growth of the free black population by decreeing that any slave liberated by his or her master must leave the state. The law symbolized not just the exhaustion of the antislavery impulse inspired by the Revolution but also a change with momentous consequences. Having existed in all the states in 1776, slavery was now an institution "peculiar" to the South.

Slavery, moreover, was deeply embedded in the new federal Constitution (even though the document did not mention it by name). Despite widespread condemnation of the African slave trade, the Constitution prohibited its abolition for twenty years. In the early years of the nineteenth century, South Carolina, where cotton production was flourishing, took advantage of this provision to import some 40,000 additional Africans. Every state was required to return fugitives, thereby making the entire nation complicitous in maintaining the system's stability. And the Constitution provided that three-fifths of the disenfranchised slave population would be counted in determining a state's representation in Congress and its allocation of electoral votes. The three-fifths clause allowed the white South to exert far greater power in national affairs than its numbers warranted. Of sixteen presidential elections between 1788 and 1848, all but four placed a Southern slaveholder in the White House.

Slavery not only survived the American Revolution but soon entered an era of unprecedented expansion. Following Eli Whitney's invention in 1793 of the cotton gin—a device that separated the cotton seed from the plant's fiber—a revolution took place in the slave system. As textile factories in England and the North consumed ever increasing supplies of cotton, slaveholders and their slaves poured into the virgin territories of the Old Southwest. After Congress prohibited the importation of Africans in 1808, a flourishing slave trade developed within the South. In the largest forced migration in American history, perhaps 1 million slaves were sold from older states like Virginia, where tobacco cultivation was in decline, to the booming Cotton Kingdom of the Deep South. On the eve of the Civil War the slave population, because of its high rate of natural increase, had grown to nearly 4 million, representing one-third of the South's total inhabitants, while in the cotton-producing states of the Deep South half the population consisted of slaves. Slavery had crossed the Mississippi River and was expanding rapidly in Arkansas and eastern Texas. The institution's center of gravity now lay not in the old centers of rice and tobacco culture on the Atlantic coast but in new states like Mississippi and Alabama.

Slave leg irons from the mid-nineteenth century. Slaves were shackled while being transported, or as a form of punishment.

"Wage Slavery"
↓
South wanted to portray evils of factories in North

←pyramid view of society
wealthy
mob.
everyone else
South's trump card when defending slavery
↓
page 9

By the 1850s Southerners seemed to have every justification for claiming that cotton was king. Three-fourths of the world's cotton supply came from the United States, mostly from the large plantations of the Gulf states, and cotton was by far the nation's most important export and source of foreign exchange. Through their financing, shipping, insuring, and consumption of the cotton crop, Northern merchants and manufacturers participated in the slave economy and shared in its profits. Indeed, while slavery retarded the South's economic development, stunting the growth of industry and urban centers, deterring immigrants from entering the region, and inhibiting technological progress, cotton-trade profits helped finance internal improvements and industrial development in the North.

The foundation of the Old South's economy, slavery powerfully shaped race relations, politics, religion, and the law. Its influence was pervasive: "Nothing escaped, nothing and no one," is one historian's assessment. This was true despite the fact that the white South was far from a monolith. The majority of white Southerners—three out of four white families in 1860—owned no slaves. Most were small farmers who lived outside the plantation belt in upcountry areas unsuitable for staple crop production and worked the land without resort to slaves or hired laborers. Unlike the planters, who produced staple crops for the world market, the South's yeomanry strove primarily for economic self-sufficiency. Even among slaveholders, the planter was far from typical. In 1850 a majority of slaveholding families owned five slaves or fewer. Less than 40,000 families possessed the twenty or more slaves that qualified them as planters.

Nonetheless, if the planter was not the "average" slaveholder or Southerner, his values and aspirations dominated Southern life. The plantation, former Maryland slave Frederick Douglass recalled after his escape to freedom, was "a little nation by itself, with its own language, its own rules, regulations, and customs." These rules and customs set the tone for all of Southern society. Ownership of slaves was the route to wealth, status, and influence. Planters not only held the majority of slaves, but controlled the most fertile land, enjoyed the highest incomes, filled state and local offices, and dominated the leadership of political parties. Despite the fact that by the 1850s the price of a "prime field hand" had risen to $2,000, well beyond the reach of most white Southerners, nonslaveholders who acquired wealth almost always invested it in land and slaves, and small slaveholders aspired to move up into the ranks of the planter class. Planter ideology glorified a hierarchical, agrarian society in which slaveholding gentlemen took personal responsibility for the well-being of their dependents—women, children, and slaves. "The master," wrote one planter, "as the head of the system, has a right to the obedience and labor of the slave, but the slave has also his mutual rights in the master; the right of protection, the right of counsel and guidance, the right of subsistence, the right of care and attention in sickness and old age." A feature of American slavery almost from

Trade card of William Boyd, a Nashville "Dealer in Negroes."

preservation of culture through struggle
— emphasis on community

Sale of Slaves and Stock.

The Negroes and Stock listed below, are a Prime Lot, and belong to the ESTATE OF THE LATE LUTHER McGOWAN, and will be sold on Monday, Sept. 22nd, 1852, at the Fair Grounds, in Savannah, Georgia, at 1:00 P. M. The Negroes will be taken to the grounds two days previous to the Sale, so that they may be inspected by prospective buyers.

On account of the low prices listed below, they will be sold for cash only, and must be taken into custody within two hours after sale.

No.	Name.	Age.	Remarks.	Price.
1	Lunesta	27	Prime Rice Planter,	$1,275.00
2	Violet	16	Housework and Nursemaid,	900.00
3	Lizzie	30	Rice, Unsound,	300.00
4	Minda	27	Cotton, Prime Woman,	1,200.00
5	Adam	28	Cotton, Prime Young Man,	1,100.00
6	Abel	41	Rice Hand, Eyesight Poor,	675.00
7	Tanney	22	Prime Cotton Hand,	950.00
8	Flementina	39	Good Cook, Stiff Knee,	400.00
9	Lanney	34	Prime Cottom Man,	1,000.00
10	Sally	10	Handy in Kitchen,	675.00
11	Maccabey	35	Prime Man, Fair Carpenter,	980.00
12	Dorcas Judy	25	Seamstress, Handy in House,	800.00
13	Happy	60	Blacksmith,	575.00
14	Mowden	15	Prime Cotton Boy,	700.00
15	Bills	21	Handy with Mules,	900.00
16	Theopolis	39	Rice Hand, Gets Fits,	575.00
17	Coolidge	29	Rice Hand and Blacksmith,	1,275.00
18	Bessie	69	Infirm, Sews,	250.00
19	Infant	1	Strong Likely Boy	400.00
20	Samson	41	Prime Man, Good with Stock,	975.00
21	Callie May	27	Prime Woman, Rice,	1,000.00
22	Honey	14	Prime Girl, Hearing Poor,	850.00
23	Angelina	16	Prime Girl, House or Field,	1,000.00
24	Virgil	21	Prime Field Hand,	1,100.00
25	Tom	40	Rice Hand, Lame Leg,	750.00
26	Noble	11	Handy Boy,	900.00
27	Judge Lesh	55	Prime Blacksmith,	800.00
28	Booster	43	Fair Mason, Unsound,	600.00
29	Big Kate	37	Housekeeper and Nurse,	950.00
30	Melie Ann	19	Housework, Smart Yellow Girl,	1,250.00
31	Deacon	26	Prime Rice Hand,	1,000.00
32	Coming	19	Prime Cotton Hand,	1,000.00
33	Mabel	47	Prime Cotton Hand,	800.00
34	Uncle Tim	60	Fair Hand with Mules,	600.00
35	Abe	27	Prime Cotton Hand,	1,000.00
36	Tennes	29	Prime Rice Hand and Cocahman,	1,250.00

There will also be offered at this sale, twenty head of Horses and Mules with harness, along with thirty head of Prime Cattle. Slaves will be sold separate, or in lots, as best suits the purchaser. Sale will be held rain or shine.

Broadside announcing a sale of slaves after the death of their owner. The advertisement notes that the slaves will be sold individually or in groups "as best suits the purchaser," an indication that families were likely to be broken up. The prices are based on the slave's sex, age, and skill.

David Walker's Appeal — compared slavery to Greek, Roman — said it was worse b/c there was no way out

Patriarchal Notion — slaves were children that needed tending

These 1867 engravings depict gangs of black men and women at work in the cotton fields. Work routines on this plantation had not changed much from antebellum days.

the outset, this paternalistic vision gained further strength after the closing of the African slave trade, which narrowed the cultural gap between master and slave and gave owners a vested interest in the survival and physical well-being of their human property. Simultaneously masking and justifying the exploitative nature of slavery, the planters' aristocratic ideals and paternalist outlook strongly affected Southern social values as a whole.

Even those white Southerners who had no direct stake in slavery shared with planters a deep commitment to white supremacy. Indeed, racism, which took as a given the idea that blacks were innately inferior to whites and unsuited for life in any condition other than slavery, was a pillar of the proslavery ideology that came to dominate the South's public life even as Northern criticism of the institution deepened. Most slaveholders found legitimation for slavery in Biblical passages such as the injunction that servants should obey their masters. Others pointed out that the ancient republics of Greece and Rome had rested on slave labor. Still others insisted that slavery guaranteed equality for whites by preventing the growth of a plebeian class doomed to a life of menial labor. Indeed, some Southerners argued that the "peculiar institution" was a more humane system of labor than the "wage slavery" that allegedly existed in the harsh market society of the North. By the 1830s fewer and fewer white Southerners shared the view, common among the founding fathers, that slavery was, at best, a "necessary evil." Increasingly they echoed the conviction of South Carolina's Senator John C. Calhoun, who, without the slightest trace of irony, called slavery "the most safe and stable basis for free institutions in the world."

For slaves, the "peculiar institution" meant a life of incessant toil, brutal punishment, and the constant fear that their families would be destroyed by sale. Before the law, slaves were property. They had few if any legal rights, could be sold or leased by their owners at will, and lacked any voice in the governments that ruled over them. Slaves could not testify in court against a white person, sign contracts or acquire property, hold meetings without a white being present, leave the plantation without permission of their owner, or be taught to read or write.

The slave, declared a Louisiana law, "owes to his master . . . a respect without bounds, and an absolute obedience." The entire system of Southern justice, from the state militia and courts down to armed patrols in each locality, was committed to enforcing the master's control over the person and labor of his slaves. Not only did the owner have the right to what Alabama's legal code called the "time, labor, and services" of his slaves, but no aspect of their lives, from the choice of marriage partners to how they spent their free time, was beyond his interference. As the nineteenth century progressed, the Southern states continued to limit the possibility of self-purchase and voluntary manumission. Few slave societies in history have so systematically closed off all avenues to freedom as the Old South.

Numbered copper tags from Charleston, South Carolina, identified slaves who had been rented by their owners to other employers. Rented slaves performed a variety of domestic, agricultural, and industrial tasks in the Old South.

First and foremost, slavery was a system of labor, and labor—"from sunup to first dark," with only brief interruptions for meals—occupied most of the slaves' time. The plantation was a diversified community, and slaves performed all kinds of work. The 125 slaves on one plantation, for instance, included a butler, two waitresses, a nurse, a dairymaid, a gardener, two carpenters, and two shoemakers. Other plantations counted among their slaves coopers, engineers, blacksmiths, and weavers, as well as a variety of domestics, from cooks to coachmen. Slaves cut wood to provide fuel for Southern steamboats, worked in iron and coal mines, laid railroad track, and constructed and repaired bridges, roads, and other facilities for local authorities. Slaves were owned by businessmen, merchants, lawyers, and civil servants, and by 1860 some 200,000 worked in industry, especially in the ironworks and tobacco factories of the Upper South. In Southern cities thousands were employed as unskilled laborers and skilled artisans. Reliance on unfree labor, moreover, extended well beyond the ranks of slaveholders, for the renting of slaves, generally for a period of one year, became an increasingly common practice.

Most slaves, of course, worked in the fields. The precise organization of their labor varied according to the crop and the size of the holding. On small farms the owner often toiled side by side with his slaves. The majority of slaves lived and worked on plantations in the cotton belt, where men, women, and children labored in gangs, often under the direction of an overseer. Among slaves, overseers had a reputation for imposing harsh treatment. "The requisite qualifications for an overseer," wrote Solomon Northrop, a free black who spent twelve years in slavery after being kidnapped from the North, "are utter heartlessness, brutality, and cruelty. It is his business to produce large crops, no matter [what the] cost." The 150,000 slaves who worked in the sugar fields of southern Louisiana also labored in large gangs. Conditions here were among the harshest in the South, for during the harvest season round-the-clock labor was required to cut and process the sugar cane before it spoiled. On the rice plantations of South Carolina and Georgia, the system of task labor prevailed. Since many of the rice planters, unlike their counterparts elsewhere in the South, were absentees, and few whites cared to venture as overseers into the disease-infested swamps in which rice was grown, blacks were assigned daily tasks and allowed to set their own pace of work. Once the daily task had been completed, slaves were free to hunt, fish, and cultivate their own crops. Workers in the rice fields enjoyed more independence than other rural slaves, although not as much as skilled urban craftsmen, who were sometimes allowed to "hire their own time" (contract individually with white employers) and even live apart from their owners.

Slaveowners employed a variety of means in attempting to maintain order and discipline among their human property. At base the system rested on force, and few slaves went through their lives without some experience of the lash.

THE NEGRO IN HIS OWN COUNTRY.

THE NEGRO IN AMERICA.

Engravings from the pamphlet Bible Defence of Slavery. *The contention that blacks were elevated and "civilized" by being brought from Africa in bondage was a centerpiece of the proslavery argument.*

Any infraction of plantation rules, no matter how minor, could be punished by a whipping; one Georgia planter recorded in his journal that he had whipped a slave "for not bringing over milk for my coffee, being compelled to take it without." Other, subtler means of control supplemented violence—exploiting and creating divisions among the slaves, especially between field hands and house servants, attempting to indoctrinate blacks in the idea of white supremacy, and creating systems of incentives that rewarded good work with monetary payments or time off.

In the face of these grim realities, slaves never abandoned the desire for freedom or the determination to resist total white control over their lives. Overcoming severe obstacles, they constructed a semi-autonomous community and culture that sustained a set of values, a worldview fundamentally at odds with that of their owners. The strength of the slave community enabled blacks to survive the ordeal of bondage without surrendering their sense of dignity and self-esteem.

At the center of the slave community stood the family. To be sure, the law did not recognize the legality of slave marriages. The master's permission was required before a man and woman could "jump over the broomstick" (the slaves' marriage ceremony), and the family stood in constant danger of being broken up through sale. Nonetheless, most slave unions, when not disrupted by sale, lasted for a lifetime. Moreover, to instill a sense of family continuity, slaves habitually named children after cousins, uncles, grandparents, and other relatives. Nor did the slave family simply mirror kinship patterns among whites. Slaves, for example, did not marry first cousins, a practice common among white Southerners. The threat of sale, with the resulting disruption of family ties, was perhaps the most powerful disciplinary weapon slaveholders possessed. For slaves, sale was a human tragedy. "My dear wife," a Georgia slave wrote in 1858,

> I take the pleasure of writing you these few [lines] with much regret to inform you that I am sold. . . . Give my love to my father and mother and tell them good bye for me, and if we shall not meet in this world I hope to meet in heaven. My dear wife for you and my children my pen cannot express the grief I feel to be parted from you all.

If the family transmitted the slave community's traditions from one generation to the next, a distinctive version of Christianity offered solace in the face of hardship and hope for liberation from bondage. Blacks, free and slave, had been swept into the South's Baptist and Methodist churches during the religious revivals of the eighteenth century known as the Great Awakening. In the nineteenth century every plantation had its black preacher, usually a "self-called" slave who possessed little formal education but whose rhetorical abilities, familiarity with the Bible, and good judgment on matters public and private made him one of the most respected members of the slave community.

To masters, Christianity offered another means of social control. Many required slaves to attend services conducted by white ministers who lectured them on the immorality of theft and the Biblical injunctions to meekness and obedience. One slave later recalled being told in a white minister's sermon "how good God was in bringing us over to this country from dark and benighted Africa and permitting us to listen to the sound of the gospel." But the slaves transformed the Christianity they had embraced and turned the gospel to their own purposes. In secret after-dark religious meetings, where the shouting, dancing, and relationship of call and response between preacher and congregation derived from African tradition, the "invisible institution" of the slave church came into its own. Blacks identified themselves as a chosen people, analogous to the Jews in Egypt of the Old Testament, whom God in the fullness of time would deliver from bondage. At the same time the figure of Jesus Christ represented to slaves a personal redeemer, one who truly cared for the oppressed. Slaves found other heroes and symbols in the Bible as well—Jonah, who overcame hard luck; David, who vanquished the more powerful Goliath; Daniel, who escaped from the lion's den. And the Christian message of brotherhood and the equality of all souls before the Creator stood as an irrefutable indictment of the institution of slavery.

Indeed, if their masters developed an elaborate ideology defending the "peculiar institution," slave culture was suffused with a sense of the unjustness of bondage. Blacks thought of themselves as a working people unjustly deprived of the fruits of their labor by idle planters who lived in luxury. "We bake de bread / they give us the crust," said a line from one slave song recalled by Frederick Douglass. Slaves' folk tales, such as the Brer Rabbit stories, glorified the weak who managed to outwit stronger foes. Their religious songs—or spirituals—spoke of lives of sorrow ("I've been 'buked and I've been scorned"), while holding out hope for ultimate liberation ("Didn't my Lord deliver Daniel?").

Confronted with federal, state, and local authorities committed to preserving slavery, and outnumbered within the South as a whole by the white population, slaves could only rarely express their desire for freedom by outright rebellion. This does not mean they placidly or contentedly accepted the system under which they were compelled to live. Resistance to slavery took many forms in the Old South, from individual acts of defiance to occasional slave uprisings.

Most widespread was "day-to-day resistance" or "silent sabotage"—doing poor work, breaking tools, abusing animals, and in other ways disrupting the plantation routine. Frederick Law Olmsted, a Northerner who toured the South in the 1850s, took note of "gates left open, rails removed from fences by the Negroes, mules lamed and implements broken, a flat boat set adrift in the river, men ordered to cart rails for a new fence, depositing them so that a double expense of labor would be required to lay them." Many slaves feigned illness to avoid work (although almost no slaves reported themselves sick on Sunday, their only day of rest). Then there was the theft of food, a form of insubordination so common that one Southern physician diagnosed it as a hereditary disease unique to blacks. Less frequent, but more threatening, were serious crimes committed by slaves, including arson, poisoning, and armed assaults against individual whites.

Even more dangerous to the stability of the slave system was running away. The obstacles confronting the prospective fugitive were indeed formidable. As Solomon Northrup recalled, "Every white man's hand is raised against him, the patrollers are watching for him, the hounds are ready to follow in his track." No one knows how many slaves reached the North or Canada, but not surprisingly, most who succeeded lived in the Upper South, especially states like Maryland, Virginia, and Kentucky that bordered on free soil. In the Deep South fugitives were more likely to make for cities like New Orleans or Charleston, where they hoped to lose themselves in the large communities of free blacks. Other escapees fled to remote areas like the Great Dismal Swamp of Virginia, or the Florida Everglades, where the Seminole Indians offered refuge to fugitive slaves. Some who escaped to the North were aided by the Underground Railroad, a loose organization of black and white abolitionists that assisted fugitives. A few individuals, like "General" Harriet Tubman, herself an escapee, made numerous forays into the South to lead slaves to freedom. But most who managed to reach the North did so on their own initiative, like Frederick Douglass, who borrowed the papers of a Maryland free black and took a train for the North, and Henry "Box" Brown, who packed himself inside a crate and literally had himself shipped to freedom.

Occasionally, resistance to slavery moved beyond such individual acts of defiance to outright rebellion. The three best-known slave conspiracies in American history occurred within the space of thirty-one years in the early nineteenth century. The first, in 1800, was organized by a twenty-four-year-old Virginia slave, Gabriel Prosser, who devised a plan for three columns of armed slaves to attack Richmond, seize the arsenal, massacre most of the white population, and possibly make for Haiti, whose slaves had recently emancipated themselves by force of arms. The plot was organized at black religious meetings, where Prosser's brother Martin, a slave preacher, related the story of the Israelites and their escape from bondage, while Gabriel cited the Declaration of Independence to condemn slavery. But the plot was discovered, and twenty-five organizers were executed.

The next major conspiracy was organized by Denmark Vesey, a slave carpenter in Charleston who had won his freedom in a lottery. An outspoken, charismatic leader, Vesey rebuked blacks who stepped off the city's sidewalks to allow whites to pass—he said they deserved to be slaves—and took a leading role in the local African Methodist church. "He studied the Bible a great deal,"

100 DOLLARS
REWARD.

Ranaway from the subscriber, on Monday June 15, a negro woman NELLY FORREST. She is about 45 years old, chunky built, large pouting mouth, good teeth, high cheek bones, walks pigeon-toed. She is slow in giving a direct answer when questioned; her manner of speaking is rather grum.

She has a free husband living on Capitol Hill, Washington City, near Sims' old rope walk, named Henson Forrest. I will give the above reward no matter where taken, so I get her again.

F. M. BOWIE,
Long Old Fields,
Prince George's County, Md.
July 6, 1857.

An advertisement seeking the return of a runaway slave. Marriages between free blacks and slaves, as described in this broadside, were not uncommon, especially in the Upper South.

A period lithograph portrays Joseph Cinquez leading a slave revolt in 1839 on the Amistad, *a Spanish schooner bound for Cuba. After the ship, under control of the slaves, reached the United States, the Supreme Court awarded the blacks their freedom and allowed them to return to Africa.*

recalled one of his followers, "and tried to prove from it that slavery and bondage is against the Bible." But like Gabriel Prosser, Vesey also drew on white America's professed ideology, quoting Jefferson's Declaration and poring over newspaper reports of the debates in Congress regarding the Missouri Compromise (1819–21). Vesey apparently devised a plan whereby slaves from nearby plantations were to attack Charleston, but in 1822 the plot was discovered. After a series of trials, thirty-five slaves and free blacks, including Vesey, were sentenced to death, and an equal number banished from the state.

The best known of all slave rebels was Nat Turner, a slave preacher and religious mystic in Southampton County, Virginia, who came to believe that God had chosen him to lead a black uprising. Turner traveled widely in the county conducting religious services. He was said to have the power to cure diseases with the touch of his hands, and he told of seeing black and white angels fighting in the sky and the heavens running red with blood. Initially Turner, with a telling sense of irony, chose July 4, 1831, for his rebellion, only to fall ill on the appointed day. On August 22 he gathered his handful of followers and led them from farm to farm assaulting the white inhabitants. By the time the militia put down the uprising, about eighty slaves had joined Turner's band and some sixty whites had been killed. Turner was subsequently captured and, with seventeen other rebels, condemned to die. Asked, before his execution, whether he regretted what he had done, he responded, "Was not Christ crucified?"

Conclusion to toned:
Opinions remained strong on racism
- Lincoln dies, no one to emancipate
↓
Blacks subject to harsh injustices
KKK rises to prominence

Among other things, these three conspiracies illustrated the central role played by the black church in the slaves' lives and the way slaves adopted for their own purposes the egalitarian values of the white society around them. Prosser's conspiracy, in addition, underscored the importance of family ties among the slaves; Vesey's revealed the close relations between free blacks and slaves; and Turner's uprising demonstrated the connection between outright rebellion and less dramatic forms of resistance, for in its aftermath numerous reports circulated of "insubordinate" behavior by slaves on Virginia's farms and plantations.

Equally revealing was the brutality with which the Prosser and Vesey plots were suppressed and the widespread panic and victimization of hundreds of innocent blacks that followed the Turner uprising. Although hardly as extensive as slave rebellions in other parts of the Western Hemisphere, which sometimes involved thousands of slaves, these events seemed to dramatize deep-seated fears that haunted the white Southern mind. The Turner rebellion, in particular, sent shock waves through the South, not only because of the number of whites killed but also because Turner himself spoke of his owner as a "good" master. "A Nat Turner," one white Virginian warned, "might be in any family." For one final time Virginia's leaders debated openly whether steps ought to be taken to do away with slavery. But instead of moving toward emancipation, the Virginia legislature of 1832 decided to fasten even more tightly the chains of bondage. New laws prohibited blacks, free or slave, from acting as preachers (a measure that proved impossible to enforce), strengthened the militia and patrol systems, and prohibited free blacks from owning firearms. Other Southern states followed suit.

In some ways the year 1831 marked a turning point for the South's "peculiar institution." The abolition of slavery in the British Empire underscored the South's growing isolation in the Western world. Turner's rebellion, following only a few months after the appearance of William Lloyd Garrison's abolitionist journal *The Liberator*, suggested that American slavery was under assault from both within and without. In response some states made membership in an abolitionist society a criminal offense, while in others critics of slavery were driven from their homes or otherwise persecuted. Antislavery societies, generally advocating "colonization" (the removal of blacks to Africa) had flourished in some parts of the South as late as the 1820s, but nearly all now died out. The South's "great reaction" produced one of the most thoroughgoing suppressions of freedom of speech in American history. For slaveholders feared that any division among the white population would encourage critics in the North and enhance blacks' own hopes for liberty.

As for the slaves, Nat Turner's was the last large-scale rebellion in Southern history. It demonstrated conclusively that in a region where whites outnumbered blacks and the white community was armed and united, slaves stood at a fatal

This 1860 view of New Orleans captures the size and scale of the cotton trade in the South's major port and largest city. More than 3,500 steamboats arrived at New Orleans in 1860.

disadvantage in any violent encounter. In the ensuing years, slaves concentrated instead on consolidating their own communities and surviving the ordeal of bondage while they waited for outside forces to alter the balance of power within the South. When they did, the slaves were ready.

In terms of slavery's geographic extent, the numbers held in bondage, and the institution's economic importance both regionally and nationally, the Old South was the largest, most powerful slave society the modern world had known. By the 1830s few white Southerners seemed willing to come to terms with a changing world or to consider seriously alternatives to their unique social order. Certainly no one could realistically believe that slavery would somehow die out of its own accord. Even as the Northern states pursued their own path of regional development and national debate over the "peculiar institution" intensified, Southern society closed in defense of slavery.

Engraved portrait of Frederick Douglass from his autobiography, published in 1845.

FREDERICK DOUGLASS
(1817–1895)

As a youth, Frederick Douglass labored as a slave in rural Maryland and in Baltimore. He knew kind masters and harsh. Recalling his desire for freedom, he later wrote: "My feelings were not the result of any marked cruelty in the treatment I received; they sprang from the consideration of my being a slave at all. It was *slavery*, not its mere incidents, that I hated."

In 1838 Douglass escaped to the North. Three years later he began to lecture for the Massachusetts Anti-Slavery Society. He soon became an internationally renowned spokesman for abolitionism and other reform movements, including women's rights. Douglass fought slavery on many fronts. He sheltered runaway slaves, edited several antislavery newspapers, and wrote an autobiography that was a powerful indictment of slavery.

During the Civil War, Douglass met many times with Abraham Lincoln, urging the president to emancipate the slaves and enlist blacks in the Union Army. He later held various public offices, including that of American ambassador to Haiti.

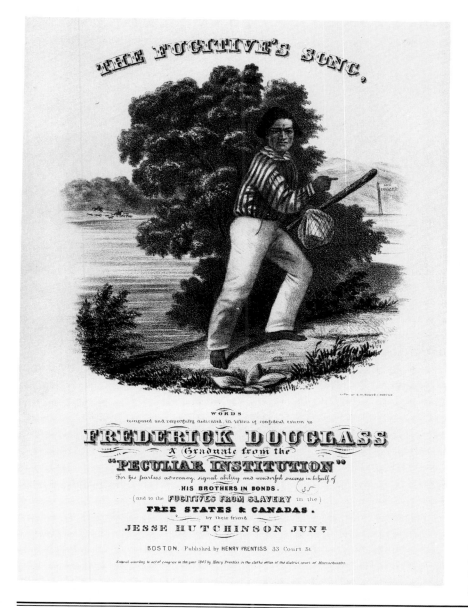

Sheet music for a song dedicated to Frederick Douglass and written by Jesse Hutchinson, a member of the famous abolitionist singing group the Hutchinson family.

An 1857 engraving of the interior of a New York City machine shop illustrates how power-driven machinery and skilled handwork could coexist in the same industrial establishment.

TWO

LINCOLN'S AMERICA

Like millions of his fellow countrymen, Abraham Lincoln grew to manhood in a society experiencing the wrenching changes brought about by westward expansion, capitalist development, and a rapidly transformed class structure. In 1809, the year of Lincoln's birth, over ninety percent of the population lived and worked on the land, mostly near the Atlantic coast. By 1860, when he was elected president, the United States had become a continental empire, and the North had been transformed into a complex market economy with booming cities and factories, a rapidly expanding commerical life, and a new laboring class.

The key to these developments was a revolution in transportation and communication. In the early nineteenth century, most roads had been little more than rutted paths through the woods. Apart from sailing ships plying the Atlantic coast and flatboats floating downstream on major rivers, trade within the new nation faced insuperable barriers. Transporting goods thirty miles inland by road cost as much as bringing the same cargo from England. It took fifty days to move goods from Cincinnati to New York City, via a flatboat ride down the Mississippi River to New Orleans and then a journey by sail up the Gulf and Atlantic coasts. America's cities mainly served as depots for foreign trade, and most manufactured goods were imported from abroad. The majority of America's farm families pursued a largely self-sufficient way of life. They produced at home most of what they consumed, from clothing to farm implements. What they could not make themselves they obtained by bartering with their neighbors or purchasing from local stores and rural artisans like blacksmiths and shoemakers.

"Let us bind the nation together, with a perfect system of roads and canals,"

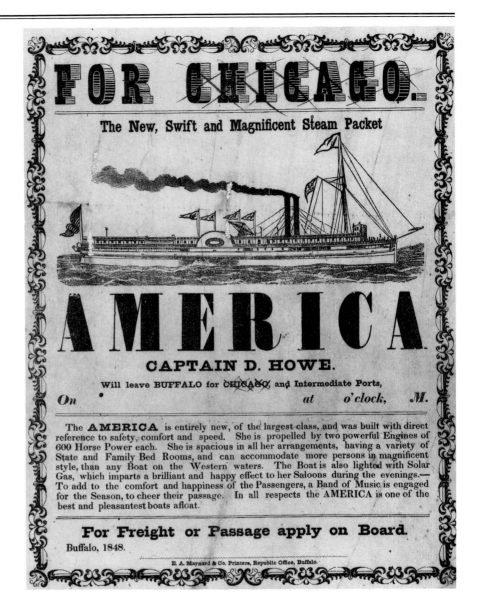

An 1848 broadside advertising a steamer on
the Great Lakes.

John C. Calhoun implored Congress in 1815, "Let us conquer space." Within
a generation, new inventions and technologies had done just that. In rapid
succession, the steamboat, canal, railroad, and telegraph pulled America out of
its underdeveloped past, opening new land to settlement, lowering transportation
costs, and creating a vast national market for economic enterprise. The steamboat, whose feasability Robert Fulton demonstrated in 1807 by navigating the
Clermont on the Hudson River, made possible upstream commerce on the

ILLINIOS CENTRAL RAILROAD.

OPEN FROM LASALLE TO BLOOMINGTON.

Arrangements commencing May 23, 1853.

Passenger Trains leave as follows, daily, (Sundays excepted):

Bloomington,	8.00 A.M.	La Salle,	2.00 P.M.
'Hudson,	8.35 "	Tonica,	2.35 "
Kappa,	8.54 "	Wenona,	3.15 "
Panola,	9.24 "	'Minonk,	3.50 "
'Minonk,	9.54 "	Panola,	4.30 "
Wenona,	10.40 "	Kappa,	5.00 "
Tonica,	11.25 "	'Hudson,	5.20 "
La Salle, arr.	12.00 "	Bloomington, arr.	6.00 "

'Stopping at these places on signal to take or leave passengers.

A Freight Train, with Passenger Car attached, will leave La Salle on Mondays, Wednesdays and Fridays at 8.30, A. M. arriving at Bloomington 2.30, P. M. stopping at all stations.

Returning, leaves Bloomington on Tuesday, Thursday and Saturday at 5 A. M. arriving at La Salle at 11 A. M.

Stages, it is expected, will soon run in connection with the Cars between Bloomington, Springfield, Decatur and Urbana.

Chicago, May 23.   **R. B. MASON, Sup't.**

This poster advertising a section of the Illinois Central Railroad illustrates how the expanding rail network opened new areas to settlement and commercial agriculture.

Mississippi, Ohio, and other major rivers, as well as rapid transport across the Great Lakes. The completion of the 364-mile Erie Canal in 1825 (a remarkable feat of engineering at a time when America's next largest canal was only 28 miles long) gave New York City primacy over competing ports in access to trade with the Northwest and set off a scramble among other states to match New York's success. Indeed, several states projected such elaborate programs of canal construction that they were unable to meet interest payments on their debt during the economic depression that began in 1837. As a result, new state constitutions of the 1840s severely limited public aid to internal improvements. By this time, however, nearly 4,000 miles of canals had been constructed, creating a network linking the Atlantic states and the Ohio and Mississippi valleys and drastically reducing the cost of transportation.

If canals supplemented existing waterways, the railroad opened vast new areas of the American interior to settlement, while stimulating the expansion of coal mining, iron manufacture, and other industries. The Baltimore and Ohio, the nation's first commercial railroad, opened in 1830. Thirty years later, 30,000 miles of track had been laid (more than existed in the entire rest of the world), with Ohio and Illinois containing the largest rail systems. The first truly modern business enterprises, trunk railroads like the Pennsylvania and New York Central, employed an army of workers and pioneered new forms of labor control and corporate management. The railroad also completed the reorientation of the Northwest's trade from the South to the East. As late as 1850, most Midwestern farmers still shipped their produce southward. Ten years later, however, nearly all their crops were transported directly east by railroad, in only two days and at a fraction of the previous cost. At the same time, the telegraph helped to make prices uniform in all parts of the country. The device was invented by Samuel F. B. Morse in 1844; within sixteen years nearly 50,000 miles of telegraph wire had been strung, making possible instantaneous communication throughout the nation.

Flowing directly from these improvements in transportation was the rise of the West. The War of 1812, which gravely weakened the Indian tribes east of the Mississippi, unleashed a flood of land-hungry settlers across the Appalachian Mountains. One stream of migration, including tens of thousands of masters and slaves, created the new Cotton Kingdom. Another consisted of farmers from the Upper South, who moved into southern Ohio, Indiana, and Illinois. A third stream flowed from New England across New York and into the Upper Northwest—Michigan, Wisconsin, and northern Ohio and Illinois. They acquired land either from the federal government, at $1.25 per acre, payable in cash, or from land speculators who offered higher prices but also long-term credit. Within a few years two new regions—the Northwest and Southwest—had entered the Union, and settlement had reached the Mississippi.

Nor did the westward movement stop here. The idea that Americans had a "manifest destiny" to occupy the entire continent was widespread even before New York editor John L. O'Sullivan coined the term in 1844. In the 1830s and 1840s hundreds of thousands of Americans made their way to Texas, Oregon, Utah, and California, before the United States enjoyed undisputed title to these areas or, in some cases, any claim to sovereignty at all. By the end of the Mexican War in 1848, the nation stretched to the Pacific, the area of settlement was five times as large as in 1800, and half the American population of 23 million lived outside the original thirteen states. Illinois, whose population grew from a mere 55,000 in 1820 to 475,000 in 1840 and 1.7 million twenty years later, when it ranked fourth among all the states, epitomized the rise of the West. Meanwhile abandoned farms dotted the New England countryside.

The process of westward expansion was not without its human cost, for the opening of the West to white settlement required the dispossession of the original inhabitants. The 1830s witnessed the end of two centuries of Indian warfare east of the Mississippi River. The last Indian resistance to the advancing tide of settlers in the Old Northwest came in 1832, when the Sauk leader Black Hawk, with about 1,000 Indians, entered Illinois to reclaim land that a faction of his tribe had previously ceded to the United States in a treaty of dubious legality. The resulting Black Hawk War pitted 7,000 militiamen, volunteers, and regular army troops against about 500 Indian warriors. The result was a devastating defeat for the Indians and undisputed white domination of the Great Lakes region. Meanwhile the federal government under Andrew Jackson and Martin Van Buren forced 85,000 Creeks, Cherokees, and members of other Indian nations to leave their tribal lands in Georgia, Alabama, Mississippi, and Florida for settlements west of the Mississippi River. The fact that many members of these so-called civilized tribes had adopted white ways, including a written language and non-Indian dress, did not protect them from removal to facilitate the onward march of the Cotton Kingdom. Most bowed to the inevitable and departed peacefully, but when the Cherokees refused to leave their ancestral homeland, federal troops evicted them. Their subsequent forced march through Georgia, Tennessee, and Missouri became known as the Trail of Tears, in which about one-quarter of the 20,000 Cherokees perished. Among Southern Indians only a portion of the Seminoles, under the leadership of Osceola, successfully resisted the U.S. Army and managed to remain in Florida.

Although the transportation revolution, westward expansion, and Indian removal occurred simultaneously in both North and South, their combined effects heightened the nation's internal divisions. Rather than spurring economic change, the South's developing transportation system remained an adjunct of the plantation economy, geared largely to transporting cotton and other staples to market. The South's expansion westward simply reproduced in the Southwest the same slave-based social order of the older states. In 1860 over 80 percent of Southerners still worked on the land. But in the North these processes set in motion an economic transformation that profoundly affected both rural and urban life.

As the frontier moved westward, the old economy of self-sufficient agriculture and rural artisanship persisted in many areas. The initial, pioneer stage of settlement reinforced the farmer's self-sufficiency, for the tasks of felling trees, building cabins, breaking the soil, and feeding the family left little time for agriculture geared to the market. But as the Northwest became a more settled

society, bound by a web of transportation and credit to Eastern centers of
commerce and banking, farmers were drawn increasingly into the new market
economy. They now concentrated on growing crops and raising livestock for
sale, and they purchased at stores goods previously produced at home. Even as
the growth of Eastern cities created increasing demand for farm products,
mortgages originating with Eastern banks and insurance companies financed
the acquisition of land on the frontier, the rapid transition to commercial
farming, and, in the 1840s and 1850s, the purchase of fertilizer and new agricultural machinery to expand production. The steel plow, invented by Illinois
blacksmith John Deere in 1837 and mass-produced by the 1850s, made possible
the rapid subduing of the resistant Western prairie soil. Virginia-born inventor
Cyrus McCormick developed the reaper in 1831, and it was produced in large
quantities soon afterward. Tens of thousands were in use on the eve of the Civil
War.

By the 1850s a new commercial empire had arisen in the Old Northwest.
Between 1840 and 1860 America's output of wheat nearly tripled, but little was
exported abroad; the bulk of the crop was consumed in the growing cities of
the East. At the same time the expanding population of Western commercial
farmers created a vast home market for Eastern manufacturers. Western cities
that stood at the crossroads of this interregional trade experienced extraordinary
growth. By 1860 Chicago, which, thanks to the railroad, controlled the commerce
of a large agricultural hinterland, had become the nation's eighth largest city.
The network of transport, credit, and commerce that bound the Northwest and
Northeast ever closer formed, one might say, the economic basis for their political
union in the Republican party of the 1850s.

Urban life was transformed no less fully than rural, as merchants, bankers,
and master craftsmen determined to take advantage of new economic opportunities created by the expanding market. In the drive to increase production
and reduce labor costs, they fundamentally altered the very nature of work. In
many trades, entrepreneurs gathered artisans into large workshops in order to
oversee their labor and subdivide their tasks. Men who traditionally manufactured a finished product like a pair of shoes or piece of furniture saw the labor
process broken down into numerous steps requiring far less skill and training.
Accustomed to setting their own pace of work, they found themselves subjected
to constant supervision by their employers and relentless pressure for greater
output and lower wages.

These changes seemed to threaten the heritage of artisan independence.
In response the late 1820s witnessed the first widespread labor organization in
American history. In major Eastern cities, journeymen alarmed at the erosion
of traditional skills and the threat of being reduced to the status of dependent
wage-earners created the world's first Workingmen's parties. In the following
decade, one of rampant inflation, union organization spread and strikes became

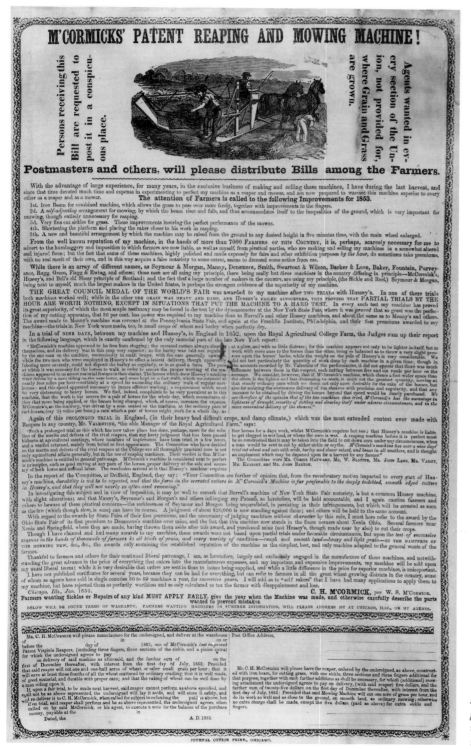

Advertising played a key role in the rapid growth of the McCormick Reaper Company, which by the 1850s was even exporting its machines abroad.

A somewhat idealized bird's-eye view of Chicago from 1858 depicts the city's thriving commercial life.

commonplace. Along with demands for higher wages and shorter hours, the labor movement of the Jacksonian era called for free public education, an end to imprisonment for debt, free homesteads on public land in the West, and other measures aimed at reaffirming the "dignity of labor" and enabling workers to resist threats to their economic independence. Some insurgent workingmen even echoed the Southern cry of "wage slavery," contending that the laboring poor of the North were no better off than the South's chattel slaves and that changes in the nature of work threatened the heritage of equal rights bequeathed by the American Revolution. Thus even as the nation's economic transformation produced an explosive growth in output and trade and a rise in the general standard of living, it simultaneously widened the gap between rich and poor, especially in the North's large cities.

In some industries, such as textiles, the factory by the 1830s and 1840s entirely superseded craft production. Like artisan workshops, factories brought together large groups of workers under central supervision, but they also replaced hand tools with power-driven machinery. The earliest factories were located along the fall line where the foothills of the Northern Appalachians met the coastal plain; here the resulting waterfalls and river rapids could be harnessed to provide power. Numerous small industrial cities arose along the fall line, from Lowell, Massachusetts, to Trenton, New Jersey. In time the application of steam power made it possible for factory owners to locate in large cities like Philadelphia and Chicago, closer to transportation and markets. By midcentury not only textiles but a wide array of other goods—tools, firearms, sewing machines, ironware, agricultural machinery—were being produced in factories. What came to be called the American system of manufactures relied on the mass production of interchangeable parts that could be rapidly assembled into standardized finished products, a technique first perfected in small-arms production. Lacking a strong internal market and available labor force, and with its slaveholding class generally disdainful of industrial development, the South lagged far behind the North in the rise of a factory system.

Since closely supervised work tending a machine seemed to violate the autonomy Americans considered an essential attribute of republican freedom, few native-born men could be induced to work in the early factories. Instead employers turned to those who had few alternative ways of earning a living. The first New England textile mills relied largely on women and children for their work force. In Lowell, Massachusetts, the most famous center of early textile manufacturing, most of the 7,000 workers tending spinning machines and power looms in the mid-1830s were young unmarried women from Yankee

In 1849 the noted lithographer Nathaniel Currier published his view of New York City, the nation's largest city and busiest port.

An advertisement for the Chicago Threshing Machine Company illustrates the city's emergence by the 1850s as a manufacturing center serving the surrounding agricultural hinterland.

farm families. Most valued the opportunity to earn money independently at a time when few other employments were open to women. "It was like a young man's pleasure in entering upon business for himself," Lucy Larcom recalled of her days at Lowell. "Girls had never tried that experiment before, and they liked it." But the "mill girls" did not constitute a permanent class of factory workers. Typically they remained in Lowell for only a few years, soon leaving to return home, marry, or move West.

Only in the 1840s and 1850s did the shortage of industrial labor ease. In those decades more than 4 million immigrants entered the country, the majority Irish refugees fleeing a devastating famine. Arriving in dire poverty and facing widespread discrimination because of their Catholicism, the Irish filled the lowest rungs of the work force, finding employment in Northern cities as day laborers and servants and taking the factory jobs native-born males shunned. Large numbers of German and Scandinavian immigrants, by contrast, generally came with the skills and economic resources that enabled them to set up as Western farmers or urban artisans and shopkeepers. Immigration fueled the rapid expansion of the North's urban centers in the mid-nineteenth century. By 1860 New York's population already exceeded 1 million (the majority of

Prevailing social ideology glorified the woman who remained at home, but economic necessity compelled many to labor in the new factories, such as this Lynn, Massachusetts, shoe manufactory depicted in 1860.

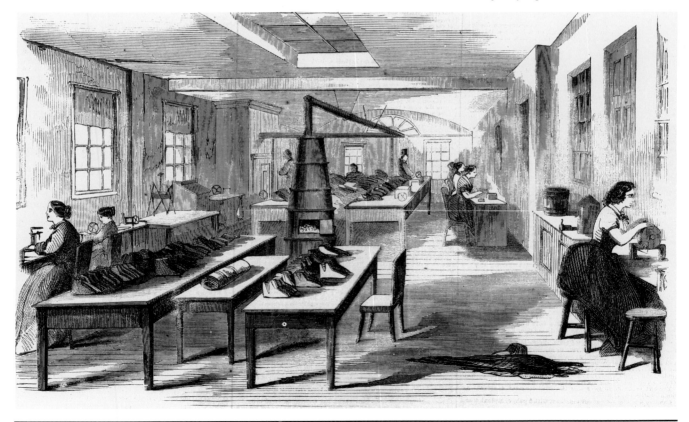

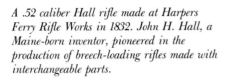

A .52 caliber Hall rifle made at Harpers Ferry Rifle Works in 1832. John H. Hall, a Maine-born inventor, pioneered in the production of breech-loading rifles made with interchangeable parts.

foreign birth), and there were ninety-three cities with populations of 10,000 (there had been only thirteen in 1820). Nearly all were located in the North. With the exception of a few large cities on its periphery, such as St. Louis, Baltimore, and New Orleans, the South remained as overwhelmingly rural as at the turn of the century.

The decline of the home as a center of economic production affected the lives of all Northerners. If increasing numbers of men left their households for paid employment outside it, many women found their traditional economic roles undermined by the availability of mass-produced goods previously made at home. Some women, as we have seen, followed work as it moved from household to factory. Others sought to adhere to a new definition of femininity, which glorified not a woman's contribution to the family's economic well-being but her ability to create an environment shielded from the disruptive impact and competitive tensions of the market economy. In the new "cult of domesticity," the outside world of paid labor and politics belonged to men, while women were to devote themselves to the domestic sphere, performing household duties and raising children to be good republican citizens. For the poor in the cities of the North this ideology had little practical meaning, for the labor of all family members, including women and children, was essential to economic survival. Apart from factory labor, thousands of poor women found jobs as domestic servants and seamstresses. But for the expanding urban middle class it became a badge of respectability for wives to remain at home, outside the disorderly new market economy.

Thus the North on the eve of the Civil War had developed a complex, interrelated economy in which Northeastern industrialists marketed manufactured goods to the commercial farmers of the West while the urban working class consumed the food Westerners produced. In a sense though, Northern society still stood poised between traditional and more modern ways of life. Although less than half the work force now labored in agriculture, the majority of the population still lived in small towns and rural areas, not large cities. Even though many more Northern farmers in the 1850s engaged in production for the market than in their fathers' and grandfathers' generations, the large majority owned their own land and still enjoyed the economic independence that came with control of productive property. Before the Civil War the full impact of the industrial revolution was felt only in New England, which by the 1850s possessed several hundred large-scale factories. Elsewhere, most manufacturing still took place in smaller towns and cities, and the typical establishment employed fewer than ten workers. A mostly immigrant class of permanent wage laborers had made its appearance, but millions of Northerners still lived and worked in the world of the craft shop and the family farm. And nearly all Northerners looked to the West as a place where they could secure their economic independence.

America's economic transformation had social and political effects that were felt as early as the 1830s. European visitors at the time marveled at a society so energetic, so materialistic, so seemingly in constant motion. Arriving in Chicago in 1835, British visitor Harriet Martineau was amazed by the prevalence of feverish land speculation. "I never saw a busier place than Chicago," she wrote. "The streets were crowded with land speculators, hurrying from one sale to another. . . . As the gentlemen of our party walked the streets, store-keepers hailed them from their doors, with offers of farms, and all manner of land-lots, advising them to speculate before the price of land rose higher." French observer Alexis de Tocqueville was struck by Americans' restless energy and apparent lack of attachment to place. "In the Untited States," he wrote in his classic work, *Democracy in America*,

> a man builds a house in which to spend his old age, and sells it before the roof is on; he plants a garden and lets it just as the trees are coming into bearing; he brings a field into tillage and leaves other men to gather the crops. . . . Thus, the Americans carry their businesslike qualities into agriculture, and their trading passions are displayed in that as in their other purposes.

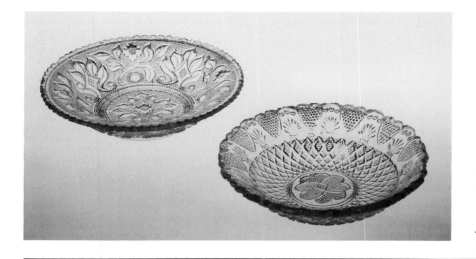

Pressed glass dishes made at the Boston & Sandwich glass factory in the 1830s. In place of earlier glass products crafted individually by skilled artisans, these were mass-produced from molds which made possible uniform patterns.

Politics, too, reflected the new age. Jacksonian politics revolved around issues spawned by the market economy's rapid expansion. Corporations, tariffs, banks, currency, land policy—these were the elements of political debate. Although both major parties—the Whigs and Democrats—were national coalitions of diverse groups with varied, sometimes contradictory approaches to the issues of the day, Democrats generally believed the government should adopt a hands-off attitude toward the economy, lest public policies award special favors to entrenched economic interests. The party attracted aspiring entrepreneurs who resented government favoritism to established businessmen, as well as numerous farmers and city dwellers suspicious of new corporate enterprises and fearful that the expansion of the market threatened to undermine their independent way of life. Whigs tended to look to the federal government to guide economic development, through protective tariffs, a national bank, and public aid for internal improvements. Most established businessmen and bankers supported this program of government promotion of economic growth, as did others who were benefiting from economic change, or hoped to do so.

The central political struggle of the Jacksonian era was the president's war against the Second Bank of the United States. A private corporation chartered in 1816 by the federal government and empowered to create a uniform national currency and oversee the operations of local banks, the bank symbolized the hopes and fears inspired by the market revolution. There had been few banks in America at the beginning of the nineteenth century, but the expanding market created a host of them, each able to issue paper currency and extend loans more or less at will. The expansion of banking helped finance the nation's economic development; but the overexpansion of currency and credit helped produce a boom-and-bust economic cycle that saw major depressions strike the country in 1819, 1837, and 1857. And the tendency of paper money to depreciate in value convinced many workers, who saw the real value of their wages in constant danger of evaporating, that bankers were "nonproducers" who contributed nothing to the nation's economy but became rich by exacting tribute from honest labor.

Furniture with machine-made parts, c. 1850. The furniture industry experienced rapid mechanization before the Civil War, making possible increased production and wider availability of fashionable styles. The rocker and sofa are believed to have come from the Springfield home of Abraham and Mary Todd Lincoln.

To Jacksonian Democrats the "Monster Bank" represented an illegitimate union of political authority and entrenched privilege, and symbolized the new unnatural concentrations of economic power created by the nation's growth. "When the laws undertake," said Jackson in his 1832 message vetoing the bank's recharter, "to grant titles, gratuities, and exclusive privileges, to make the rich richer and the potent more powerful, the humble members of society—the farmers, mechanics, and laborers . . . have a right to complain of the injustice of their government." To Whigs the bank was an essential means of guiding the process of economic change. But Jackson's effective appeal to popular values helped him win a sweeping reelection victory in 1832.

The market's logic also affected politics in ways unrelated to specific partisan issues. By the 1840s both major parties were "selling" their candidates through massive rallies and a flood of banners, badges, and broadsides. Political leaders like Andrew Jackson and Henry Clay (Whig senator from Kentucky) emerged as folk heroes complete with distinctive nicknames (in these cases, Old Hickory and Harry of the West). The manipulation of campaign imagery reached its height in 1840, when the Whigs for the first time captured the White House by portraying William Henry Harrison as the "log cabin" candidate and running him without a platform. This marketing device bore little relation to the wealthy Harrison's actual life but resonated strongly with popular values. At the same time modern forms of party organization arose based on local machines headed by men for whom politics was a profession and whose main preoccupation was getting out the vote on election day. The new party machines ushered in a great expansion of mass involvement in politics. With the end of most property qualifications for voting (although racial and sexual barriers remained), nearly all white men were able to cast ballots. They did so in record numbers—nearly eighty percent of those eligible voted in the election of 1840. The humble origins of the presidents of the 1830s—Jackson was born on the North Carolina frontier and orphaned as a youth, his successor Martin Van Buren was the son of a Kinderhook, New York, tavernkeeper—contrasted sharply with the wealthy backgrounds of earlier presidents, reflecting how politics had come to embody Americans' democratic, egalitarian aspirations.

In a heterogeneous nation whose two major sections were following divergent paths of regional development, the national political parties, uniting men of all backgrounds and from all parts of the country in pursuit of common goals, formed powerful bonds of union. Yet they could play this role only so long as the problem of slavery remained outside national politics.

A poster from 1840 illustrates the campaign imagery employed to great effect by the victorious Whigs.

William Henry Harrison's "Log Cabin" campaign of 1840 generated an abundance of campaign material, including this tortoise-shell log cabin.

This daguerreotype of Lincoln was taken at the time of his election to Congress in 1846.

ABRAHAM LINCOLN
(1809–1865)

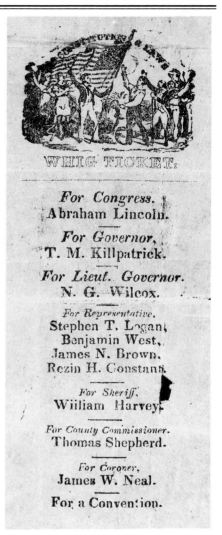

The early life of Abraham Lincoln typified experiences shared by millions of Northerners.

Lincoln's family moved west from Kentucky to Indiana in 1816, partly, he later said, "on account of slavery," which restricted the economic prospects of non-slaveholding whites. In 1830 Lincoln moved farther west, settling in New Salem, Illinois, where he worked as a clerk in a general store. Two years later he volunteered for the Illinois militia in the Black Hawk War but saw no action.

Like many of his contemporaries, Lincoln in the 1830s sought personal advancement through politics. He served as a Whig member of the Illinois legislature (1834–1842), campaigned actively for his party's presidential candidates, and was elected to a single term in Congress in 1846.

After leaving office in 1849, Lincoln earned his livelihood from an increasingly successful law practice. By the 1850s, the self-educated Lincoln was one of Illinois' most prominent attorneys, representing, among other clients, the powerful Illinois Central Railroad.

Lincoln believed his own life exemplified the virtues of the North's free labor system. In the South, laborers were "fatally fixed in that condition for life," but in the North, he declared, opportunities for "advancement, improvement in condition," and economic independence existed for every individual.

An election ticket listing Whig candidates for various Illinois offices in 1846, including Abraham Lincoln for Congress.

This engraving depicts the 1837 attack on abolitionist editor Elijah P. Lovejoy's office that resulted in his death.

THREE

THE SLAVERY CONTROVERSY

As early as the debates over the Declaration of Independence and the Constitution, slavery had been a divisive issue. And in the first three decades of the nineteenth century, despite the best efforts of party leaders to exclude it from national debate, the question of slavery occasionally came to the forefront of politics. When Missouri in 1819 sought admission to the Union as a slave state, it set off two years of controversy over whether the South's "peculiar institution" should be allowed to expand into Western territories. The crisis was finally resolved by the Missouri Compromise, engineered by Senator Henry Clay. The compromise admitted Missouri along with the free state of Maine (to preserve the political balance between North and South), while barring slavery from lands north of latitude 36'30"—nearly all the remaining territory belonging to the United States.

A decade later South Carolina attempted to nullify the tariff of 1828—that is, prevent its enforcement within the state's borders—sparking a dangerous political impasse resolved by another compromise. Although not the ostensible issue, slavery played a major role in producing the Nullification Crisis, for many Southern leaders feared that the rapidly growing North might one day use its influence in the federal government to weaken the institution. To prevent such an eventuality, John C. Calhoun, retreating from his earlier nationalist position, sought to cripple the power of the federal government by elaborating a theory of state sovereignty. In ratifying the Constitution, Calhoun insisted, the states had ceded some of their authority to Washington, but each retained the right to abrogate federal policies that threatened its vital interests. He argued that key issues should be resolved not by simple majority rule, which would allow the more populous North to control national policy, but by a "concurrent majority," with each major region or economic interest (such as slaveholders and manufacturers) able to veto measures that threatened its well-being. Although South Carolina received little support from other Southern states during the Nullification Crisis, Calhoun's political theories soon acquired widespread popularity within the South, and states rights became a crucial bulwark in the defense of slavery.

But more than anything else, what made slavery a focus of national debate was the rise in the 1830s of the abolitionist movement. Abolition was only one part of the multifaceted reform impulse that emerged in these years. Americans established organizations devoted to preventing the manufacture and sale of liquor, ending the delivery of the mails and other "frivolous" activities on Sunday, improving conditions in prisons, alleviating the plight of the blind, insane, and poor, renouncing war as a means of settling disputes among nations, expanding educational opportunities, and reorganizing society on a communitarian basis. These reformers differed in their tactics: communitarians such as the followers of European Socialists Robert Owen and Charles Fourier, established their own settlements in the hope of demonstrating by example the superiority of a collective way of life, while many opponents of "the demon rum" sought to use the power of government to force recalcitrant drinkers to change their ways. But all these groups sent out speakers, gathered signatures on petitions, published pamphlets, and strove to convert public opinion to their cause.

Many of these reform movements drew their inspiration from the Second Great Awakening, a wave of religious revivalism that swept over large parts of the country in the 1820s and 1830s. The revivalist preachers rejected older Calvinist ideas of original sin and predestination in favor of an emphasis on each individual's ability to achieve salvation through an exercise of free will. "God has made man a moral free agent," proclaimed Charles G. Finney, the most prominent revivalist preacher. Sin was voluntary, and men and women could be convinced to change their ways. The revivals made popular the outlook known as "perfectionism," which considered both the individual and society itself capable of indefinite improvement. Indeed, once saved, the devout man or woman was expected to help root out sin from society at large.

One man's "sin," of course, is another's pleasure, and revivalism and its ensuing reform movements aroused considerable hostility among those who rejected the idea that one group of Americans had the right to impose moral standards upon its neighbors. Those, for example, who enjoyed Sunday recreation or a stiff drink from time to time did not think they were any less moral than teetotlers who had been "reborn" at a religious camp meeting. Others insisted that problems like poverty had roots in the structure of society rather than the "sinfulness" of poor people. But the vision of a society freed from sin

During the 1830s and 1840s, abolitionist societies sponsored agents to lecture publicly on the evils of slavery. "No Union with Slaveholders" was a motto of followers of William Lloyd Garrison, who advocated disbanding the Union because of slavery.

'And I will make with them a covenant of peace, and will cause the evil beasts to cease out of the land, and they shall dwell safely in the wilderness, and sleep in the woods.' *Ezekiel 34: 25*

CAMP MEETING.

'The wilderness and the solitary place shall be glad for them, and the desert shall rejoice and blossom as the rose.' *Isaiah 35: 1*

became the driving force behind the reform impulse of the 1830s, pushing older, moderate movements in a new, radical direction. Under the impact of the revivals, temperance became prohibitionism, criticism of war became outright pacifism, and a new movement arose devoted to the immediate and total abolition of slavery.

There was nothing new, of course, in the idea that slavery represented an affront to God's will, human rights, and American values. Before 1830, however, the most prominent vehicle for antislavery sentiment in the United States had been the American Colonization Society. Founded in 1816, with a membership that included numerous business leaders and virtually every major political figure from Andrew Jackson to Henry Clay, the society believed slavery could be eliminated only with the cooperation of slaveholders and that racial prejudice was so deeply embedded in American life that blacks and whites must be

The lithograph, Camp Meeting, *evokes the spirit of mid-nineteenth-century religious revivalism.*

permanently separated. It advanced a program of gradual abolition coupled with the resettlement of emancipated slaves in West Africa. The result would be an America free of both slavery and the black presence. In the North the society attracted many individuals sincerely convinced of the evil of slavery; in the South, however, it seemed to devote most of its energy to persuading free blacks to leave the country.

The abolitionist movement that arose in the 1830s differed profoundly from its genteel, conservative predecessor. Drawing on the moral conviction that slavery was an unmitigated evil and the secular one that it contradicted the

This Wells printing press is believed to have been used by Elijah P. Lovejoy, abolitionist editor of the Alton Observer.

values enshrined in the Declaration of Independence, a new generation of abolitionists rejected the colonization approach and demanded immediate emancipation. They directed strident, explosive language against slavery and slaveholders and insisted that blacks, once free, should not be deported but incorporated as equal citizens of the republic. Perfecting American society meant rooting out not only slavery, but racism in all its forms.

The most prominent leaders of the antislavery movement of the 1830s were William Lloyd Garrison and Theodore Dwight Weld. The appearance in 1831 of *The Liberator*, Garrison's weekly journal published in Boston, is usually taken to mark the emergence of the new breed of abolitionism. "I will be as harsh as truth," he announced, "and as uncompromising as justice. On this subject, I do not wish to think, to speak, or to write with moderation. . . . I will not equivocate—I will not excuse—I will not retreat a single inch—and I will be heard." And heard he was, partly because Southerners, outraged by his inflammatory rhetoric (one editorial called slaveowners "an adulterous and perverse generation, a brood of vipers"), reprinted his editorials in their own newspapers in order to condemn them, thus providing Garrison with instant notoriety. Some of Garrison's ideas, such as the proposal that the North abrogate the Constitution and dissolve the Union to end its complicity in the evil of slavery, were rejected by many abolitionists. But *The Liberator* remained the preeminent antislavery journal.

If Garrison was the movement's most notable propagandist, Weld, a young minister who had been converted by Finney, helped create its mass constituency. Himself a brilliant orator, Weld trained a band of seventy speakers, who brought the abolitionist message into the heart of the rural North. Their methods were those of the revivals—fervent preaching, protracted meetings, calls for individuals to renounce their immoral ways—and their text a simple one: slavery was a sin. "In discussing the subject of slavery," wrote Weld, "I have always presented it as preeminently a moral question, arresting the conscience of the nation. As a question of politics and national economy, I have passed it with scarce a look or a word." There was far more to this approach than a concern for religious morality. Identifying slavery as a sin with which compromise was inadmissible was essential if the strategy of gradualism was to be discredited and along with it the idea that some middle ground could be found between slavery's continued growth and its outright abolition. And the moral condemnation of slavery flowed as well from the conviction that enslaved blacks were prospective citizens being deprived of their natural rights, rather than an inferior caste who could never be successfully incorporated into American society.

Many Southerners feared that the abolitionists' ultimate aim was to set off a slave insurrection, a belief strengthened by the outbreak of Nat Turner's rebellion a few months after *The Liberator* made its appearance. Yet not only was Garrison's newspaper completely unknown to Turner, but the abolitionists, despite their

Lucretia Coffin Mott, a Quaker abolitionist and advocate of women's rights, was one of the nineteenth century's most prominent reformers. In this daguerreotype from around 1850 she is wearing a Quaker bonnet and shawl.

Sojourner Truth, born a slave in New York State around 1797, was widely known for her lectures on spiritualism and abolitionism.

militant language, rejected violence as a means of ending slavery. Many, indeed, were pacifists or "nonresistants" who believed coercion should be eliminated from all human relationships and institutions. "Moral suasion" was their strategy: slaveholders must be convinced of the sinfulness of their ways, and the North of its complicity in the peculiar institution. (Some critics at the time charged that this approach left nothing for the slaves to do in seeking their own liberation but await the nation's moral regeneration.) Standing outside established institutions, abolitionists adopted the role of radical agitators. Among the first to appreciate the key role of public opinion in a mass democracy, they focused their efforts not on infiltrating the existing political parties but on awakening the nation to the moral indignity of slavery. Their language was deliberately provocative, calculated to seize public attention. "Slavery," said Garrison, "will not be overthrown without excitement, without a most tremendous excitement."

Beginning with a handful of activists, the abolitionist movement spread rapidly throughout the North. Antislavery leaders seized upon the recently invented steam press to produce literally millions of pamphlets, newspapers, and broadsides. Between the formation of the American Anti-Slavery Society in 1833 and the end of the decade, some 100,000 Northerners joined local societies devoted to abolition. Most were ordinary citizens—farmers and merchants in rural areas, craftsmen and other laborers in the cities. And much of the movement's grass-roots strength derived from the women who joined by the thousands. Women organized abolitionist meetings, circulated petitions, and sometimes delivered public lectures. Not a few, in working for the rights of the slave, developed a new understanding of, and resentment against, their own subordinate social and legal status.

Angelina and Sarah Grimké, the daughters of a prominent South Carolina slaveholder, were pioneers in the women's movement. Having converted first to Quakerism and then abolitionism, they offered in their popular lectures a scathing condemnation of slavery from the perspective of those who had witnessed its evils firsthand. When clergymen, outraged by the sight of females sacrificing all "modesty and delicacy" on the public lecture platform, denounced the sisters, the Grimkés turned to speaking and writing on women's issues: first the right of women to take part in political debate, and then their right to share the social and educational privileges enjoyed by men. The sisters soon retired from the fray, but when the first organized movement for women's rights arose in the 1840s, its leaders borrowed the language of equal rights and the organizational techniques of abolitionism. The key organizers of the Seneca Falls Convention of 1848, which raised the issue of women's suffrage for the first time, were Elizabeth Cady Stanton and Lucretia Mott, both veterans of the antislavery crusade.

From its inception, blacks also played a leading role in the antislavery movement. Even before the appearance of *The Liberator*, Northern free blacks

Engravings from the original 1852 edition of Uncle Tom's Cabin.

had organized in opposition to the Colonization Society. In 1829 David Walker, a free black living in Boston, published the pamphlet *Walker's Appeal*, a searing indictment of slavery whose uncompromising language and demand for immediate abolition anticipated Garrison's approach. "Tell us no more about colonization," Walker declared, "for America is as much our country as it is yours." James Forten of Philadelphia, a successful black sailmaker, helped finance *The Liberator* in its early years, and many of the journal's first subscribers were Northern blacks, attracted by Garrison's rejection of colonization and his demand for equal rights for black Americans. Several blacks served on the board of directors of the American Anti-Slavery Society, and Northern-born blacks and fugitive slaves quickly emerged as major organizers and speakers.

Frederick Douglass was only one among many former slaves whose published accounts of their lives in bondage convinced thousands of Northerners of the evils of slavery. Indeed, the most effective piece of antislavery literature of the entire period, Harriet Beecher Stowe's novel *Uncle Tom's Cabin*, was to some extent modeled on the autobiography of fugitive slave Josiah Henson. Serialized in 1851 in a Washington antislavery newspaper and published as a book the following year, *Uncle Tom's Cabin* had sold over 1 million copies by 1854, and was performed in numerous stage versions. By portraying slaves as sympathetic men and women, Christians at the mercy of slaveholders who split up families and set bloodhounds on innocent mothers and children, Stowe's melodrama gave the abolitionist message a powerful human appeal.

The first racially integrated social movement in American history and the first to give equal rights for blacks a central place in its political agenda, abolitionism was nonetheless a creature of its time and place. Racism was endemic in nineteenth-century America, North as well as South. The 220,000 blacks living in the free states (composing less than 2 percent of the North's population) suffered discrimination in every phase of their lives, and racist imagery became the stock in trade of such popular entertainments as minstrel shows. Most Northern blacks lived in the poorest, unhealthiest sections of cities like New York, Philadelphia, and Cincinnati. Only a handful of states allowed blacks to vote, and none accorded them what today would be considered full equality before the law. In Illinois, for example, blacks could not vote, testify or sue in court, serve in the militia, or attend public schools. In 1853 the legislature even prohibited any black person from entering the state, a measure also adopted by four other Northern states between 1840 and 1860.

White abolitionists could not free themselves entirely from this pervasive prejudice. They monopolized the key decision-making posts, black spokesman Martin R. Delany charged, relegating blacks to "a mere secondary, underling position." Yet what is remarkable is not that white abolitionists reflected the prejudices of their society but the extent to which they managed to rise above them. Not only did they struggle to overturn Northern laws discriminating

Racist caricatures of blacks illustrated the covers of popular antebellum sheet music. "Jim Crow" and "Zip Coon" were both published in the 1830s.

against blacks, but they refused to compromise the principle that the slave was a moral being, created in the image of God. The abolitionist emblem—a portrait of a slave in chains coupled with the motto, "Am I Not a Man and a Brother?"—challenged white Americans to face up to the reality that men and women no different from themselves were being held in bondage.

Initially, abolitionism aroused violent hostility from Northerners who feared it threatened to disrupt the Union, interfere with profits wrested from slave labor, and overturn white supremacy. Led by "gentlemen of property and standing"—often merchants with close commercial ties to the South—mobs disrupted abolitionist meetings in numerous Northern cities. In 1835 a Boston crowd led Garrison through the streets with a rope around his neck, and the editor barely escaped with his life.

Two years later, the movement acquired its first martyr when antislavery editor Elijah P. Lovejoy was killed by a mob in Alton, Illinois, while defending his printing press. A native of Maine and a licensed Presbyterian minister, Lovejoy had begun his editorial career in the slave state of Missouri but was

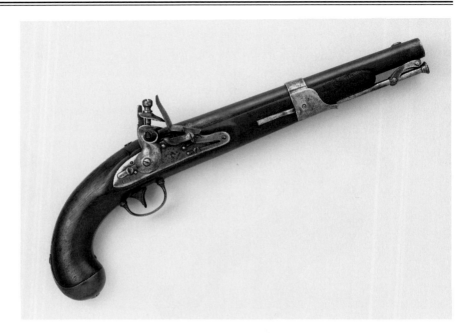

Although percussion weapons were available at the time of the Mexican War, the military preferred flintlock guns, like this .54 caliber pistol made by Simeon North.

soon forced to flee to Illinois. In Alton, then the state's largest city, with numerous Southern-born residents and a flourishing trade with the South, Lovejoy's message that "the system of Negro slavery is an awful evil and sin" won few converts. Four times mobs destroyed his printing press, only to see Lovejoy resume publication; the fifth attack ended in his death.

Elsewhere crowds of Southerners, with the tacit approval of Andrew Jackson's Postmaster General Amos Kendall, burned abolitionist literature removed from the mails. And in 1836 the House of Representatives attempted to stem the flood of abolitionist petitions by instituting the notorious "gag rule," which provided that future petitions regarding slavery would automatically be tabled without discussion. The rule remained in effect until 1844, when it was repealed, thanks largely to the tireless opposition of former President John Quincy Adams, who now represented Massachusetts in Congress.

Far from stemming the growth of the movement, however, mob attacks and attempts to limit abolitionists' freedom of speech invigorated it. Moreover, these events generated sympathy for the movement by convincing many Northerners that slavery was not only morally repugnant but incompatible with the democratic liberties of white Americans. "We commenced the present struggle," announced abolitionist William Jay, "to obtain the freedom of the slave; we are compelled to continue it to preserve our own. We are now contending . . . for the liberty of speech, of the press, and of conscience." The abolitionist movement was subtly broadening its appeal in a way that resonated with the beliefs of many Northerners who cared little about the rights of blacks but could be convinced that slavery endangered their own cherished freedoms.

Although abolitionism remained a significant presence in Northern public life until emancipation was achieved, by 1840 the movement had accomplished its most important work. In that year disputes over issues ranging from the wisdom of running abolitionist candidates for public office to the proper role of women in antislavery work had caused abolitionism to split into two wings. But by this time, with over 1,000 local antislavery societies scattered throughout the North, the movement had created a broad constituency awakened to the moral issue of slavery. Perhaps the abolitionists' greatest achievement was to shatter the conspiracy of silence that had sought to preserve national unity and make intersectional politics possible by suppressing public discussion of slavery.

In the 1840s slavery moved to the center stage of American politics. It did so, however, not in the moral language or with the immediatist program of abolitionism but as a consequence of the nation's territorial expansion and Northerners' growing determination that the new Western lands be preserved as "free soil." In 1845 the Senate approved the annexation of Texas, which had won its independence from Mexico in the previous decade, adding a vast new slave region to the nation. Then President James K. Polk, determined to acquire California and other provinces of Mexico, instigated the Mexican War. Although the majority of Americans—inspired by the expansionist fever of manifest destiny—supported the war, a significant minority dissented, fearing that far from expanding the "great empire of liberty," the administration aimed to obtain new lands for slavery. The American victory resulted in a treaty ceding nearly 1 million square miles—half of Mexico's national territory—to the United States. But the acquisition of this vast area raised the fatal issue that would disrupt the political system and eventually plunge the nation into Civil War: whether slavery should be allowed to expand into the West. Events soon confirmed Ralph Waldo Emerson's prediction that, if the United States gobbled up part of Mexico, "it will be as the man swallows arsenic. . . . Mexico will poison us."

Why did the slavery issue come to focus not on abolition in the states where the institution existed but its extension into new territories? "Free soil" had a popular appeal in the North that far exceeded the abolitionists' demand for immediate emancipation and equal rights for blacks. As a legal position free soil was persuasive, for while Congress possessed no constitutional power to abolish slavery within a state, venerable precedents existed for keeping territories free from slavery. Congress had done this in 1787 in the Northwest Ordinance and again in the Missouri Compromise. The idea of preventing the creation of new slave states also appealed to those who favored policies, such as the protective tariff and government aid to internal improvements, that the majority of Southern political leaders opposed. For thousands of Northerners, moreover, the ability to move to the new Western territories held out the promise of economic betterment, of maintaining or reestablishing that economic independence threatened by wage labor in the East. Were slave plantations to occupy the most fertile

The Mexican War became a popular subject for artists like Nathaniel Currier, who printed an abundance of inexpensive lithographs such as The Battle of Sacramento. *U.S. troops are charging from the left against Mexicans on the right.*

Decorative plates adorned the tall, slender hats, known as shako caps, of American forces in the Mexican War. The design of an eagle with military weapons reflected the ebullient spirit of manifest destiny.

lands of the West, Northern migration would be effectively blocked. The free soil idea also accommodated the racism so widespread in Northern society. Association with blacks, whether free or slave, it was said, would degrade white labor; far preferable to preserve the territories for white settlers.

To white Southerners, of course, the idea of barring slavery from territory acquired from Mexico seemed a palpable violation of their equal rights as members of the Union. After all, Southerners had fought and died to win these territories; surely they had a right to share in the fruits of victory. For the federal government to single out slavery as the one form of property barred from the West would be an affront to the South and its distinctive way of life. Just as Northerners viewed westward expansion as essential to their economic well-being, Southern whites believed that slavery must expand or die. The expansion of slavery was not simply an issue: it was a central fact of the nation's experience since the Revolution. A majority of slaves in 1850 lived in states that had not even existed when the Constitution was adopted. Slavery, it seemed, needed virgin lands to thrive. Moreover, the admission of new free states in the West would overturn the delicate political balance between the sections and make the South a permanent minority. Southern interests would not be secure in a Union dominated by nonslaveholding states.

The divisive potential of the issue of slavery's expansion became clear in 1846, when Pennsylvania Congressman David Wilmot proposed a resolution prohibiting slavery from all territory acquired from Mexico. In the House vote, party lines crumbled as every Northerner but two supported the Wilmot Proviso, while nearly all Southerners, Democrat and Whig, opposed it. The measure passed the House, where the more populous free states possessed a majority, but failed in the Senate, with its even balance of free and slave states. But, said one newspaper, the proviso, "as if by magic, brought to a head the great question that is about to divide the American people." Two years later, opponents of slavery's expansion organized the Free Soil party and nominated Martin Van Buren for president and Charles Francis Adams as his running mate. Van Buren polled some 300,000 votes in the 1848 election, fourteen percent of the Northern total, and his campaign gave a great impetus to the spread of antislavery feeling. The fact that a former president and the son of another were willing to abandon their respective parties to run on a free soil platform showed that opposition to slavery had spread far beyond abolitionist ranks. "Antislavery," commented New York Senator William H. Seward, "is at length a respectable element in politics."

To this serious threat to party stability, established political leaders reacted as they had for decades: they moved to resolve outstanding differences between the sections and expel slavery from national political debate. In 1850 Henry Clay proposed a compromise to settle a series of issues in dispute between North and South. California, which had formed a constitution, would be ad-

1 Henry Clay.	5 William H. Seward	9 John C. Calhoun.	13 Stephen A. Douglas	17 William R. King,	21 Willie P. Mangum	25 Jeremiah Clemens
2 Daniel Webster.	6 Millard Fillmore.	10 James A. Pearce	14 Pierre Soule,	18 John Bell,	22 Samuel Houston,	26 Arthur P. Butler.
3 Thomas H. Benton,	7 William L. Dayton,	11 Robert F. Stockton	15 Truman Smith	19 James M. Mason	23 John P. Hale,	27 John Davis.
4 Lewis Cass,	8 William M. Gwin.	12 Henry S. Foote.	16 Salmon P. Chase.	20 James Cooper,	24 Asbury Dickens,	28 Dodge. (Wis.)

An engraved image of Henry Clay proposing the Compromise of 1850 to the U.S. Senate. Also visible are Daniel Webster, Stephen A. Douglas, and John C. Calhoun.

mitted to the Union as a free state. The slave trade, but not slavery, would be abolished in the nation's capital. A stringent new law would allow Southerners to reclaim slaves who had escaped from bondage, without even offering accused fugitives the right to a jury trial. And the status of slavery in the remaining territories acquired from Mexico would be left to the discretion of the inhabitants, with no interference from outside, a policy that soon became known as popular sovereignty.

In the dramatic Senate debate on the compromise, the divergent sectional positions received eloquent expression. Calhoun, too ill to speak and only a few weeks from his death, had a colleague read a speech rejecting the very idea of compromise. Slavery, he insisted, must be protected by the national government

Portrait of Black Hawk *by Homer Henderson, a late nineteenth-century American artist, after a portrait painted in 1837 by Charles Bird King. Black Hawk wears a feather headdress, wampum necklace and earrings, and a medal depicting an unknown government agent.*

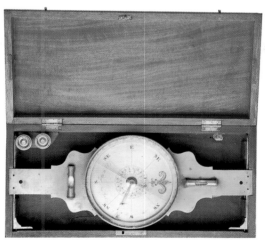

A brass surveyor's compass used on the Great Plains in the late 1840s.

An American Slave Market, *painted in 1852 by the unknown artist Taylor, depicts the sale of a runaway slave, "George." Two years earlier, Congress had enacted the Fugitive Slave Law, which greatly strengthened the means for recapturing runaway slaves.*

Eyre Crowe, an English artist traveling in America in 1853, painted After the Sale: Slaves Going South from Richmond. *In the foreground, two men dicker over the sale as slaves are loaded onto a wagon. Richmond was one of the South's leading centers of slave trading.*

Harriet Beecher Stowe, author of Uncle Tom's Cabin, *portrayed in an 1853 engraving produced in London.*

Made in England shortly after his death, this ceramic plate commemorates Elijah P. Lovejoy as "The First Martyr to American Liberty."

This portrait of Henry Clay, painted on a wooden panel, is believed to be the work of Kentucky painter Matthew H. Jouett around 1825.

John C. Calhoun, prominent South Carolina statesman and advocate of states' rights, portrayed by American artist John Lambdin around 1845.

Lincoln's nickname, "The Railsplitter," recalled his humble origins. An unknown artist used the image to create a larger-than-life portrait, which depicts the White House in the distance. The painting is believed to have been displayed at campaign rallies in 1860.

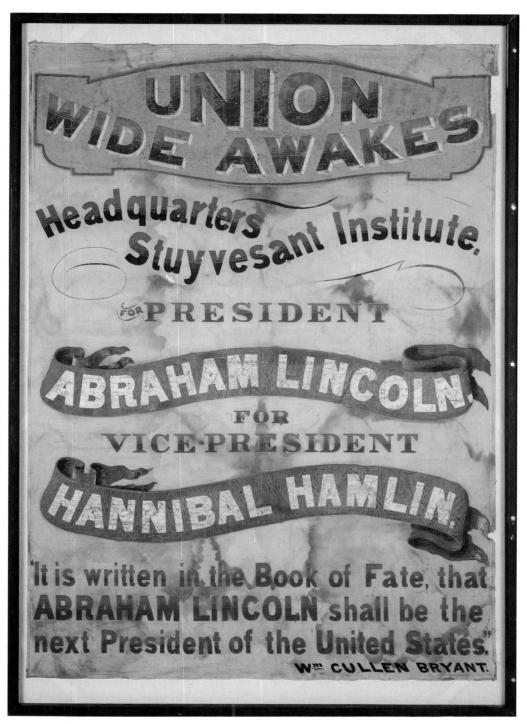

This banner, which quotes poet and editor William Cullen Bryant, was used by the "Wide Awakes," a Republican campaign organization that paraded through New York and other cities with torches, lanterns, flags, and banners.

A handstitched silk militia flag from Saluda, South Carolina, featuring a figure reminiscent of George Washington on horseback, illustrates how Southern secessionists often compared their cause to the American struggle for independence.

and extended into all the territories, and the balance between slave and free states must at all costs be maintained. As the stronger region the North must yield, or the Union could not survive. A week later William H. Seward also opposed compromise. The North, he declared, was growing more powerful and populous every day; no artificial political equilibrium could be maintained, and slavery must be barred from the territories. To claims of the South's constitutional rights, Seward responded that a "higher law"—the law of morality—condemned slavery. Here was the voice of abolitionist moralism and Northern self-confidence, now represented in the U.S. Senate.

Daniel Webster, senator from Massachusetts and spokesman for the Union, by an unknown artist, c. 1845.

Powerful voices, however, spoke for compromise. Clay delivered an impassioned speech for the Union, and Daniel Webster of Massachusetts expressed his willingness to abandon the Wilmot Proviso and even accept a new fugitive slave law if this were the price of sectional peace. In the end, Clay's compromise was adopted, although not in its original form as a single measure but as a series of individual bills, shepherded through Congress by Senator Stephen A. Douglas of Illinois. Each measure passed by adding a small group of procompromise congressmen to one or the other sectional voting bloc. This was hardly an auspicious way to settle the crisis, since it indicated that relatively few members of Congress were devoted to compromise per se. But for the last time political leaders had succeeded in mobilizing their resources to expel the dangerous slavery question from national debate, even though the new Fugitive Slave Law was a recipe for further controversy. The law prompted thousands of Northern blacks to flee to safety in Canada, while others violently resisted capture in a series of dramatic confrontations. But the compromise seemed to have restored sectional peace and party unity, at least temporarily.

Not until 1854 did the old political order finally succumb to the disruptive pressures of sectionalism. Early that year Douglas introduced a bill to provide territorial governments for Kansas and Nebraska. A strong advocate of Western development, Douglas believed these territories could never be brought into the Union as states, nor could a transcontinental railroad be constructed through them, unless they were insulated from the slavery controversy. This he hoped to accomplish by applying to them the principle of popular sovereignty embodied in the Compromise of 1850. Unlike the Mexican Cession, however, Kansas and Nebraska lay in the nation's heartland and were ripe for settlement; moreover, slavery had been barred from both by the Missouri Compromise, which Douglas's bill repealed. A group of antislavery congressmen quickly issued the *Appeal of the Independent Democrats*, one of the most effective pieces of political persuasion in American history. The appeal arraigned Douglas's bill as a "gross violation of a sacred pledge," part and parcel of "an atrocious plot" to convert free territory into a "dreary region of despotism, inhabited by masters and slaves." It helped convince millions of Northerners that the Slave Power aimed at nothing less than extending the peculiar institution throughout the entire West.

In the wake of Douglas's Kansas-Nebraska Act, American politics underwent the most profound reorganization in the nation's history. The Whig party was torn apart, tens of thousands of Northerners abandoned the Democrats, and a new organization, the Republican party, came into existence, dedicated to prohibiting the expansion of slavery. Further muddying the political waters was the meteoric rise, and equally dramatic decline, of the Native American or Know-Nothing party, which was devoted to restricting immigration (especially of Catholics) and reserving officeholding to native-born citizens. In some states the Know-Nothings moved effectively to fill the vacuum created by the collapse of the Whigs, and for a time it was not clear whether opposition to the expansion of slavery or hostility to foreigners and Catholics would form the basis of the nation's second major party.

By 1856, however, the same slavery issue that had disrupted the old parties had destroyed the Know-Nothings as a national institution. Republicans managed to convince most Northerners that the Slave Power posed a more immediate threat to their liberties and aspirations than "popery" and immigration. The new party's appeal rested on the conviction that the North's social order was superior to that of the South. In contrast to the energetic, progressive, democratic North, the South represented decadence, stagnation, and aristocracy. Slavery was the cause, for it spawned a social order consisting of degraded slaves, poor whites with no hope of advancement, and idle oligarchs. The salient quality of Northern society, by contrast, was the opportunity it offered the laborer to achieve economic independence. Thus, to Republicans the slavery issue was as much a matter of "social and political economy" as a moral imperative. The struggle over the territories was really a contest over which of two fundamentally antagonistic social systems would dominate the West and, by implication, the nation's future. Slavery must be kept out of the territories so that free labor could flourish.

Their "free labor ideology," which resonated so effectively with deeply held Northern values, helps explain the Republicans' rapid rise to prominence. But their ascent was also abetted by events in 1855 and 1856. When civil war broke out in Kansas between settlers from free and slave states, the violence fueled the party's growth. Republicans also drew strength from a dramatic incident in the halls of Congress, when South Carolina Representative Preston Brooks, wielding a gold-tipped cane, beat antislavery Senator Charles Sumner of Massachusetts unconscious. In the election of 1856 the new party, although failing to elect its candidate, John C. Frémont, carried eleven of the sixteen free states and forty-five percent of the North's total vote, a remarkable achievement for an organization that had existed for only two years.

Thirty years earlier, in the aftermath of the Missouri controversy, Martin Van Buren had noted that the national political parties formed an important "antidote" to sectional loyalties and prejudices by "producing counteracting

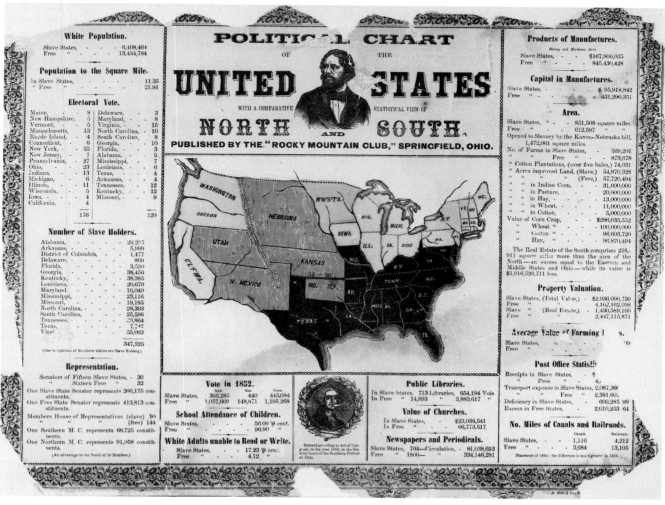

An 1856 chart graphically illustrates the division between slave and free states. John C. Frémont, Republican presidential candidate, is pictured at the top.

feelings." The 1856 election returns made starkly clear that a sectional line had been drawn across the nation's politics. One major party had been destroyed, another seriously weakened, and a new one had arisen, devoted entirely to the interests of the North. If the precarious national party system disintegrated, could the Union itself long survive?

Portraits of John and Mary Jones painted around 1865 by Chicago artist Aaron E. Darling.

JOHN JONES
(c. 1816–1879) and
MARY RICHARDSON JONES
(1819–1910)

In 1845 John and Mary Jones, free blacks from the South, moved to Chicago, where John Jones established a tailor shop. By 1860 he had become one of the nation's wealthiest free blacks and a nationally known abolitionist.

Mary Jones worked with her husband. Their home served as a haven for fugitive slaves and a meeting place for abolitionists, including Frederick Douglass and John Brown. She was also active in the woman suffrage movement.

John Jones's greatest achievement came in 1865 with the repeal of the Illinois Black Laws. For seventeen years he had lobbied against these statutes, which prohibited blacks from settling in Illinois and from serving on juries and testifying in court against whites.

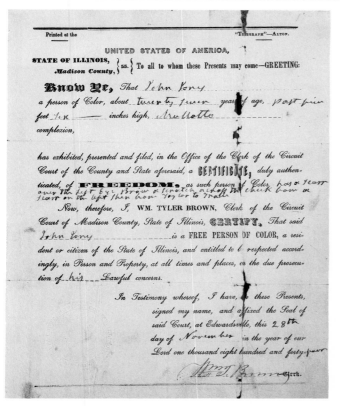
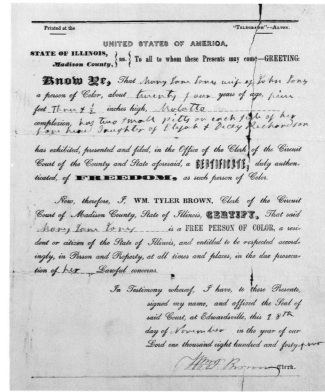

These "Certificates of Freedom," issued by Illinois in 1844 to John and Mary Jones, allowed them to live and work in the state.

These laws, Jones argued, violated fundamental democratic principles that concerned whites as well as blacks: "It is not the complexion or shades of men we are discussing; it is the right of all . . . the interest of one is the interest of all."

After the Civil War, Jones was one of the first blacks to win elective office in the North, serving as a member of the Cook County Board of Commissioners.

Currier and Ives's lithograph, Bombardment of Fort Sumter, *depicts the attack by Confederate batteries that launched the Civil War.*

FOUR

THE IMPENDING CRISIS

In the late 1850s the American people faced their greatest crisis as the slavery question tore the nation apart. The final collapse of the party system took place during an administration whose chief executive epitomized the old political order. Born during Washington's presidency, James Buchanan had served in Pennsylvania's legislature, both houses of Congress, and as secretary of state under James K. Polk. A staunch believer in the Union and upholder of the Constitution, Buchanan set out to insulate national politics from the slavery issue and pacify inflamed sectional emotions. Few presidents have failed more disastrously in what they aimed to accomplish.

Even before his inauguration, Buchanan became aware of an impending Supreme Court decision that promised to settle the slavery controversy once and for all. This was the case of Dred Scott, the slave of Dr. John Emerson, a citizen of Missouri. During the 1830s Scott had lived with Dr. Emerson in Illinois, where slavery was prohibited by state law, and in the Wisconsin Territory, where the Missouri Compromise barred it. After returning to Missouri, Scott sued for his freedom, claiming that residence on free soil had made him free.

The Dred Scott decision, announced in March 1857, two days after Buchanan's inauguration, hinged on three questions. Could a black person be a citizen and therefore sue in federal court? Did residence in a free state free Scott? Did Congress possess the power to prohibit slavery in a territory? Speaking for a court divided 6–3 (with Justice Robert C. Grier of Pennsylvania, at Buchanan's urging, joining a five-man Southern majority), Chief Justice Roger A. Taney ruled that only white persons could be citizens of the United States, since the nation's founders believed blacks "had no rights which the white man was bound to respect." The case could have ended there, but Taney, like Buchanan, was mesmerized by the idea of resolving the slavery issue entirely. In his opinion the chief justice argued that Scott remained a slave, since Illinois law was not applicable after his return to Missouri, and as for Wisconsin, Congress possessed no power to bar slavery from a territory. The Missouri Compromise, and by implication any measure interfering with the right of Southerners to bring their slave property into the territories, was unconstitutional. The decision, a Georgia newspaper exulted, "covers every question regarding slavery and settles it in favor of the South." In effect the Supreme Court had declared the platform of the nation's second largest party a violation of the Constitution.

Perhaps the person least directly affected by the Dred Scott decision was the plaintiff himself, for a new master immediately emancipated Scott and his wife Harriet. (Both died on the eve of the Civil War, having enjoyed their freedom for only a brief moment.) The impact on the political system was more far-reaching. Among the decision's casualties was the reputation of the court itself, which in the North sank to the lowest level in all of American history. Rather than altering their opposition to the expansion of slavery, Republicans denounced the court as a handmaiden of the Slave Power. The decision also seemed to undermine Douglas's doctrine of popular sovereignty, for if Congress lacked the power to prohibit slavery in a territory, how could a legislature created by Congress do so? But Douglas refused to abandon a policy that he believed embodied Americans' commitment to democracy and local self-government.

Slavery, announced President Buchanan, henceforth existed in all the territories, including Kansas, "by virtue of the Constitution." And in 1858 his administration attempted to admit Kansas as a slave state, under the Lecompton Constitution, which had been drafted by a pro-Southern convention and never submitted to a popular vote. Outraged by this violation of popular sovereignty, Douglas joined in an unlikely alliance with congressional Republicans to block the attempt. The Lecompton battle made bitter enemies of Buchanan and Douglas and convinced Southern Democrats that they could not trust their party's most popular Northern leader. Even after the immediate controversy faded, the administration continued a vendetta against Douglas, attempting to sabotage his reelection campaign in 1858 and then stripping him of the chairmanship of the Senate Committee on the Territories.

The depth of Americans' divisions over slavery were brought into sharp focus in the Lincoln-Douglas campaign of 1858. Seeking reelection to the Senate as both a champion of popular sovereignty and the man who had prevented the administration from forcing slavery upon the people of Kansas, Douglas faced an unexpectedly strong challenge from Abraham Lincoln, then little known outside Illinois. Until the mid-1850s Lincoln's career hardly seemed destined

Engraved portraits of Dred and Harriet Scott in 1857, just after the Supreme Court ruled against Dred Scott's claim to citizenship and freedom.

Abraham Lincoln as he appeared in 1858, the year of the Lincoln–Douglas debates.

for greatness. He had served four relatively undistinguished terms as a Whig in the state legislature and sat in Congress from 1847 to 1849 (when his criticism of the Mexican War was so unpopular that it was blamed for the election of a Democrat to succeed him). From 1849 to 1854 he turned his back on politics, pursuing a lucrative career as a lawyer.

As with many men for whom the traditional party system seemed to have no room, Lincoln was swept back into politics by the Kansas-Nebraska Act. Lincoln was no abolitionist, but he had long been more willing to criticize slavery than most Illinois politicians. In 1837, when a resolution condemning the abolitionists and affirming the South's right to property in slaves passed the legislature by an overwhelming margin, Lincoln and another member issued a protest: "[We] believe that the institution of slavery is founded on both injustice and bad policy; but that the promulgation of abolition doctrines tends rather to increase than to abate the evil." Hardly a ringing condemnation of slavery, this was still an unpopular position for an up-and-coming politician to take.

Unlike most abolitionists, Lincoln revered the Union and the Constitution and was willing to compromise with the South on many issues to preserve them. "I hate to see the poor creatures hunted down," he once wrote of fugitive slaves, "but I bite my lip and keep silent." Lincoln, moreover, shared many of the racial prejudices of his day and accepted without challenge its racial proscriptions. Yet, as he wrote, he "hated slavery, I think as much as any abolitionist," and on one question he was inflexible: the nonextension of slavery.

Beginning in 1854 Lincoln developed a critique of slavery and its expansion that epitomized the central values of the emerging Republican party and the millions of Northerners whose loyalty it commanded. His speeches combined the moral fervor of the abolitionists with the respect for order and the Constitution of more conservative Northerners. "I hate it," he said of the prospect of slavery's expansion, "because of the monstrous injustice of slavery itself. I hate it because it deprives our republican example of its just influence in the world— enables the enemies of free institutions, with plausibility, to taunt us as hypocrites—causes the real friends of freedom to doubt our sincerity." But, he added, "for their tardiness in [emancipation], I will not undertake to judge our brethren of the South." Lincoln effectively invoked free-labor values in his critique of slavery. His own career exemplified what an individual born in poverty could achieve in the North, where, according to the free-labor view, the opportunity for economic independence beckoned to all. The slave, of course, had no such prospect. "I want every man to have the chance," said Lincoln, "and I believe a black man is entitled to it, in which he *can* better his condition."

It was the senatorial campaign against Douglas, the North's preeminent political leader, that created Lincoln's national reputation. In accepting his party's nomination in June 1858, Lincoln etched sharply the differences between them, partly in order to undercut Douglas's new reputation—gained through the Lecompton battle—as an opponent of the South. "A house divided against itself," he announced, "cannot stand. I believe this government cannot endure, permanently half *slave* and half *free*." Lincoln's point was not that civil war was imminent but that Americans must choose between favoring or opposing slavery. Douglas's Kansas-Nebraska Act and policy of popular sovereignty, he insisted, had replaced the founding fathers' commitment to the "ultimate extinction" of slavery with a moral indifference that could only result in the institution's expansion throughout the entire country.

The seven Lincoln–Douglas debates, conducted through the fall up and down the state, remain classics of American political oratory. Douglas insisted that a heterogeneous nation could survive only by keeping divisive issues out of politics and by respecting the right of each locality to determine its own institutions. He declared, moreover, in response to Lincoln's famous Freeport Question, that the Dred Scott decision had not invalidated popular sovereignty. A territorial legislature might lack the power to prohibit slavery directly, but by failing to afford the "peculiar institution" police protection, a territory could effectively make it impossible for slaveholders to settle there. Douglas also defended his much-quoted statement, "I do not care whether slavery is voted up or down," against Lincoln's charge of amoralism. What Douglas meant was that the politician had no right to impose his own moral standards on society as a whole. In a critique not only of the antislavery movement but of the entire reform impulse deriving from religious revivalism, Douglas declared:

> I deny the right of Congress to force a slaveholding state upon an unwilling people. I deny their right to force a free state upon an unwilling people. I deny their right to force a good thing upon a people who are unwilling to receive it. . . . You must allow the people to decide for themselves whether it is a good or an evil.

Of course, when Douglas spoke of "the people," he meant whites alone. Douglas spent much of his time in the debates attempting to portray Lincoln as a dangerous radical whose positions threatened to degrade white Americans by reducing them to equality with blacks. American nationality, he insisted, had a racial definition: blacks were an inferior caste, and Jefferson in the Declaration of Independence had no intention of suggesting that they were entitled to the rights to life, liberty, and the pursuit of happiness.

Lincoln took great pains to appear moderate during the debates. He denied seeking repeal of the Fugitive Slave Law and rejected Douglas's charge that he favored political equality between the races: "I am not, nor ever have been, in favor of making voters or jurors of Negroes, nor of qualifying them to hold office, nor to intermarry with white people." But Lincoln also challenged Douglas's attempt virtually to exclude blacks from the human family; no less than whites, they were entitled to the inalienable rights of Jefferson's Declaration. Fundamentally, Lincoln insisted that local autonomy might suffice for ordinary political questions, but slavery was so transcendent a concern that its future must be determined by a national decision, not a series of local ones. As the debates continued, Lincoln increasingly moved to the moral level of the slavery controversy: "Everything that emanates from [Douglas] or his coadjutors, carefully excludes the thought that there is anything wrong with slavery. . . . If you do admit that it is wrong, Judge Douglas can't logically say that he doesn't care whether a wrong is voted up or down."

The returns revealed that Illinois, like the nation itself, was divided into two regions with sharply divergent political cultures: southern Illinois, settled

John Brown in the 1850s.

from the South and strongly Democratic, and the more rapidly growing northern part of the state, firmly in the Republican column. Narrowly winning reelection, Douglas believed he had demonstrated how to beat back the Republican challenge and had positioned himself for a successful run for the White House in 1860. Indeed, his victory was all the more remarkable because in other Northern states Republicans swept to victory in 1858. Resentment over the administration's Kansas policy, coupled with the impact of an economic depression that began in 1857, produced the defeat of twenty-two of the fifty-three Northern Democratic congressmen and Republican victories even in states—like Indiana and Pennsylvania—that Buchanan had carried two years before.

By now, however, Douglas's position on slavery in the territories was no more acceptable to the South than Lincoln's. Abandoning the principle of local autonomy that had been one of the bulwarks of the defense of slavery, Southern political leaders demanded that Congress establish and protect the peculiar institution in every territory. It was a logical consequence of the Dred Scott decision, they insisted, that if a territory failed to protect slave property Congress had an obligation to do so. This was a position that virtually no Northern politician could accept; for the South to insist on it would guarantee the destruction of the Democratic party as a national institution.

In 1859, sectional tensions grew worse when the abolitionist John Brown launched an armed assault on the federal arsenal at Harpers Ferry, Virginia.

John Brown used this Bible while in prison after his capture at Harper's Ferry. He marked passages that justified taking violent action against injustice.

An engraving of John Brown's raid on Harper's Ferry, published in Frank Leslie's Illustrated Newspaper *three weeks after the event.*

Brown had a long career of involvement in abolitionist activities. In the 1830s and 1840s he had befriended fugitive slaves and, although chronically short of money, had helped to finance black antislavery publications. Like many other abolitionists, Brown was a deeply religious man who read the Bible every day and prayed frequently. But his God was not the revivalists' forgiving Jesus, who encouraged sinners to save themselves through conversion, but the vengeful father of the Old Testament. Slavery, Brown believed, was nothing less than a state of war, and only violence could do away with it. By the mid-1850s, in the wake of armed resistance to the capture of fugitive slaves, civil war in Kansas, and bloodshed on the Senate floor, Brown was not the only abolitionist to believe that the strategy of "moral suasion" must be superseded by more direct tactics. He alone, however, plotted violent action to overthrow slavery.

As early as 1847 Brown had outlined to Frederick Douglass a plan to establish a military base in the mountains of western Virginia from which he would liberate slaves and conduct guerrilla operations against the state militia. This idea was temporarily set aside in 1855, when Brown and a number of his sons embarked for Kansas. In May 1856, after proslavery settlers burned the free-soil town of Lawrence, Brown and six other men murdered five proslavery settlers at Pottawatomie Creek. For the next two years he traveled through the North and Canada, raising funds and enlisting followers for his war against slavery. On October 16, 1859, with eighteen men, five of them black, Brown seized the arsenal at Harpers Ferry. The band was soon surrounded and captured by a detachment of Marines headed by Lieutenant Colonel Robert E. Lee. Two men escaped; ten were killed; and seven, including Brown, were captured and subsequently executed.

Although Brown's raid appeared to pose little threat to slavery, the reactions to it widened the gulf between North and South. Placed on trial for treason to the state of Virginia, Brown conducted himself with dignity and courage, winning admiration from millions of Northerners who did not necessarily approve of his violent deeds. His final speech to the court was an eloquent statement of his creed:

> I deny everything but what I have all along admitted—the design on my part to free the slaves. . . . Now, if it is deemed necessary that I should forfeit my life for the furtherance of the ends of justice, and mingle my blood . . . with the blood of millions in this slave country whose rights are disregarded by wicked, cruel, and unjust enactments—I submit, so let it be done.

When Virginia's governor spurned pleas for clemency, Brown became a martyr in the eyes of many Northerners, a symbol of the heroic individual who takes dramatic action in a moral cause. Henry David Thoreau pronounced him "a crucified hero," and on the day of his execution church bells tolled in communities throughout the North. Brown's last letter was a brief, prophetic statement: "I, John Brown, am quite certain that the crimes of this guilty land will never be purged away but with blood."

Like Nat Turner's rebellion, Brown's raid inspired a wave of hysteria within the South, even though not a single slave had joined the insurrection. Many white Southerners considered the raid irrefutable proof of what they had claimed for thirty years—that the abolitionist movement planned to incite a slave rebellion. Brown's failure seemed less significant than the adulation with which he was viewed by much of the Northern public. The raid, defenders of slavery feared, was only a portent of what the South could expect if Republicans gained control of the national government.

With the Republicans continuing to gain strength in the North, Democrats might have been expected to put a premium on party unity as the election of 1860 approached. By this time, however, a sizable group of secessionists had concluded that Southern prospects were far more encouraging outside the Union than within it. Throughout the 1850s, influential writers and political leaders in the South kept up a drumbeat of complaints about the mistreatment of their section. The North, they charged, reaped the benefits of the cotton trade, while

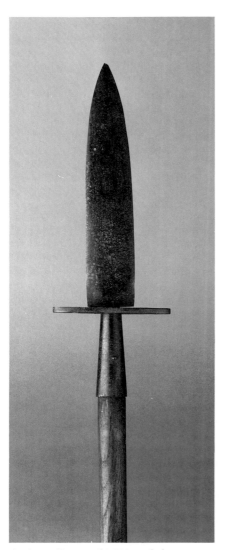

An iron pike, one of 1,000 made by a Connecticut blacksmith on contract to John Brown. Brown planned to use the pikes to arm rebellious slaves.

JOHN BROWN

Meeting the Slave mother and her Child on the steps of Charlestown jail on his way to execution.

The Artist has represented Capt Brown regarding with a look of compassion a Slave-mother and Child who obstructed the passage on his way to the Scaffold. — Capt Brown stooped and kissed the Child — then met his fate.

FROM THE ORIGINAL PAINTING BY LOUIS RANSOM.

John Brown was memorialized in America and abroad as an antislavery martyr. Bronze medals issued in France shortly after his execution recall Brown and his companions as, "dead victims of their devotion to the cause of liberty for blacks." The lithograph, John Brown Meeting the Slave Mother and Her Child, *by Currier and Ives, was based on a painting by Louis L. Ransom.*

Abraham Lincoln, Republican candidate for president, photographed by Alexander Hesler on June 3, 1860.

Southerners fell deeper and deeper into debt. To remain in the Union was to accept an inferior status. But an independent South could become the foundation of a slave empire ringing the Caribbean and embracing Cuba, other West Indian islands, Mexico, and parts of Central America. By the late 1850s some Southerners were calling for the reopening of the African slave trade, hoping that an influx of new slaves would increase the number of whites with a vested interest in the institution and lay the groundwork for slavery's expansion southward. And by early 1860 seven states of the Deep South had gone on record demanding that the Democratic platform pledge to protect slavery in all the territories of the United States. Few Southern nationalists had any illusion that Democrats would unite on such a program, but many hoped the demand would split both the party and the country and produce an independent Southern Confederacy.

At the Democratic convention in April 1860, Douglas's supporters commanded a majority, but not the two-thirds required for a presidential nomination. Because of his fight against Kansas's Lecompton constitution and his refusal to support a congressional slave code for the territories, Douglas was now anathema to leading Southerners. When the convention adopted a platform reaffirming the doctrine of popular sovereignty, delegates from seven slave states walked out, and the gathering recessed in confusion. Six weeks later it reconvened, replaced the bolters with Douglas supporters, and nominated him for president. In reaction a group of Southern Democrats placed their own ticket in the field, headed by John C. Breckenridge of Kentucky.

The Democratic party, the last great bond of national unity, had been shattered. National conventions had traditionally been places where party managers, mindful of the need for unity in the fall campaign, had reconciled their

A photograph of an August 8, 1860, Republican campaign rally in Springfield, Illinois, in front of the Lincoln home. Lincoln can be seen, dressed in a white suit, standing to the right of the front door.

PROGRESSIVE DEMOCRACY_PROSPECT OF A SMASH UP.

A Republican political cartoon by Currier and Ives from 1860 ridiculed Douglas and Southern Democratic candidate John C. Breckinridge.

differences. But in 1860 neither Northern nor Southern Democrats were interested in conciliation. In the South, an important segment of the party either favored disunion or refused to countenance any compromise that might lead to the containment of slavery. Other Southern Democrats no longer trusted their Northern counterparts, or viewed them as politically too vulnerable to be relied on to protect Southern interests. Douglas's backers, for their part, would not accept a platform that doomed their party to certain defeat in the North. They were willing, moreover, to tolerate a Southern walkout that would leave the party firmly under their own control. Even if 1860 produced a Republican victory, they expected Douglas to reach the White House in 1864 at the head of a reunited Democratic party.

The Republicans meanwhile gathered at Chicago and chose Lincoln as their standard-bearer. Lincoln entered the convention with less support than William H. Seward of New York, but Seward suffered from significant liabilities. Former Know-Nothings, a majority of whom had by now joined the Republican ranks, bitterly resented Seward's efforts as governor of New York to conciliate Irish voters by channeling state funds to parochial schools. (Like Seward, Lincoln had refused to ally himself with the nativists and had encouraged foreign-born voters to join the Republican party; but former Know-Nothings preferred him to the hated New Yorker.) Then, too, Seward had a not entirely deserved reputation for radicalism as a result of his "higher law" speech of 1850 and another in 1858 that characterized differences between North and South as an "irrepressible conflict."

In part because he was less well-known, Lincoln had a more moderate image than Seward, although as one who had often stressed the moral dimension of the sectional controversy he was acceptable to Republicans from abolitionist backgrounds. Most important, with his base in Illinois Lincoln seemed better positioned to carry the "doubtful states" of the lower North so essential for Republican victory. Added to these considerations were more mundane ones: Lincoln's convention managers promised cabinet posts to leading Republicans from Pennsylvania and Indiana, swinging these undecided delegations to support his candidacy. Lincoln was nominated on the third ballot. The platform denied the validity of the Dred Scott decision, reaffirmed Republicans' intention of prohibiting slavery's expansion, and included economic planks that appealed to a broad array of Northern voters and were opposed by the South—free homesteads for settlers on federal land in the West, a protective tariff, and government aid in building a transcontinental railroad.

In effect 1860 witnessed two presidential campaigns, one in each section. In the North, Lincoln and Douglas were the protagonists. Douglas campaigned as the last of the great compromise politicians, the heir of Clay, Webster, and other spokesmen for the political center. The Republicans, confident of victory, organized parades, caravans, and mass meetings under the banner of the Wide Awake Clubs. They emphasized how their candidate's rise from log cabin to the threshold of the White House epitomized the opportunities free society ostensibly offered each citizen, no matter how humble his origins. In the South the Republicans had virtually no presence, and three candidates contested the election: Douglas, Breckenridge, and John Bell of Tennessee. Devotion to the Constitution was the platform of Bell's hastily organized Constitutional Union party, and his candidacy appealed mainly to Southerners not yet ready to embrace secession.

The most striking thing about the election returns was their sectional character. Lincoln carried the entire North, receiving 1.8 million votes (fifty-four percent of the region's total) and 180 electoral votes. Breckenridge captured most of the slave states, although Bell won three states of the Upper South and about forty percent of the Southern vote as a whole. Douglas placed first only in Missouri, but his 1.3 million votes were second in number only to Lincoln's. Douglas was the only candidate with significant support in all parts of the country—a vindication, in a sense, of his effort to transcend sectional divisions. But his defeat suggested that a traditional career for the Union was no longer possible by 1860. Without a single ballot in ten Southern states, Lincoln was

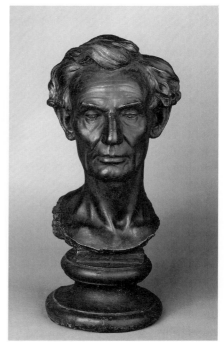

Leonard Volk sculpted this bust in the spring of 1860, while Lincoln was in Chicago arguing a legal case. Volk later recalled that during the sittings Lincoln told "some of the funniest and most laughable of stories."

Lincoln's life mask and hands were cast in bronze from plaster molds by Chicago sculptor Leonard W. Volk in 1860.

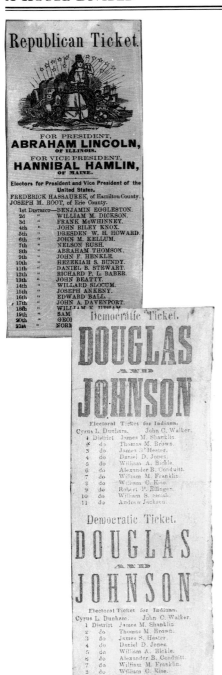

Election tickets for each of the four parties in the 1860 presidential election.

elected the nation's sixteenth president. He received only forty percent of the total vote, but would still have been elected even if all the votes of his opponents had been cast for a single candidate. Lincoln's victory was not the result of division among his opponents; rather it demonstrated how the American electoral system enabled a party to capture the presidency by concentrating its votes in the most populous section of the country.

More than seventy years before the secession crisis, James Madison had explained how local autonomy could coexist with a powerful central government in a large, heterogeneous republic. The nation's very diversity of interests, he argued in *The Federalist*, offered security to local rights, for no one interest could ever gain control of the government; every majority would be a coalition of minorities. In the 1830s, John C. Calhoun recognized the danger the antislavery movement posed for slaveholders: it threatened to rally the North upon a single principle antithetical to the interests of the minority South. By 1860 Calhoun's fear had been realized. In the eyes of many Southerners, Lincoln's election violated the rules that were supposed to govern American politics. To accept his victory would be to place the future of slavery at the mercy of a party avowedly hostile to Southern values and interests. Those advocating secession did not believe Lincoln's administration would take immediate steps against slavery in the states (although it would certainly act to prevent slavery's expansion). But if, as seemed possible, the election of 1860 marked the beginning of a long period of Republican rule, who could say what the North's antislavery sentiment would demand in five years, or ten? Slaveowners, moreover, feared Republican efforts to extend their party into the South, appealing to nonslaveholding whites, reviving the long suppressed internal debate on the future of slavery, and inspiring hopes of deliverance among the slaves themselves. Rather than accept permanent minority status in a nation governed by their opponents, Southern political leaders boldly struck for their region's independence. What was at stake, they believed, was not a single election but an entire way of life.

In the months that followed Lincoln's victory, seven states of the Cotton Kingdom, stretching from South Carolina to Texas, seceded from the Union. First to act was South Carolina, the state with the highest percentage of slaves in its population, and with a long history of political radicalism. The legislature's *Declaration of the Immediate Causes of Secession* placed the preservation of slavery squarely at the center of the crisis: the North had "assumed the right of deciding upon the propriety of our domestic institutions"; Lincoln was a man "whose opinions and purposes are hostile to slavery"; and "experience has proved that slaveholding states cannot be safe in subjection to nonslaveholding states." The declaration concluded, "There can be but one end by the submission of the South to the rule of a sectional antislavery government at Washington . . . the emancipation of the slaves of the South."

As the Union unraveled, many Americans struggled to find a formula that would resolve the crisis. Senator John J. Crittenden of Kentucky, a slave state on the border between North and South, offered the most widely supported compromise proposal of the secession winter. Embodied in a series of unamendable constitutional amendments, Crittenden's plan would have prohibited virtually all action by the federal government regarding slavery and extended the Missouri Compromise line to the Pacific Ocean, dividing between slavery and free soil all territories "now held, or hereafter acquired." The Deep South rejected the compromise as too little, too late. But many in the Upper South and North saw it as a viable way to settle sectional differences and prevent secession from spreading further.

The Crittenden plan foundered, however, on the opposition of Abraham Lincoln. Willing to conciliate the South on many issues, Lincoln was inflexible on the expansion of slavery; on that question, he informed one Republican leader, he intended to "hold firm, as with a chain of steel." A fundamental principle of democracy, Lincoln believed, was at stake. "We have just carried an election," he wrote a Republican congressman, "on principles fairly stated to the people. Now we are told in advance that the government shall be broken up unless we surrender to those we have beaten, before we take the offices. . . . If we surrender, it is the end of us and the end of the government." Moreover,

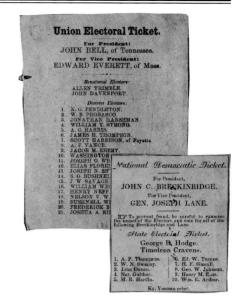

A Richmond cartoonist in April 1861 satirized Lincoln's attempt to restrain Virginia from joining the Southern states fleeing the Union's grasp.

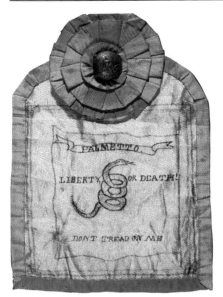

A secessionist cockade, or ribbon, repeating the revolutionary era motto, "Don't Tread on Me." Southerners wore cockades on their hats and coats to show support for secession.

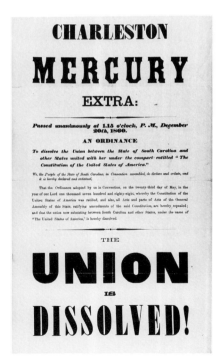

A newspaper extra edition, dated December 24, 1860, announcing South Carolina's secession.

Lincoln feared that the phrase "or hereafter acquired" offered the South a thinly veiled invitation to demand the acquisition of Cuba, Mexico, and other territory suited to slavery. To adopt the compromise thus promised a future of unending agitation. In his House Divided speech, Lincoln had predicted that for the sectional controversy to be resolved, "a crisis must be reached and passed." Now that the crisis had come, a compromise would do nothing more than put off the inevitable day of reckoning.

Before Lincoln assumed office on March 4, 1861, the seven seceding states formed the Confederate States of America, adopted a constitution, and chose for their president Mississippi Senator Jefferson Davis, one of the South's largest slaveholders and most prominent political leaders. With a few alterations—the president served a single six-year term, cabinet members (as in Britain) could sit in Congress, and the president could veto individual items in appropriation bills—the Confederate constitution was closely modeled on that of the United States. It departed from the federal constitution, however, in mentioning slavery explicitly. The Confederate constitution prohibited Congress from impairing the right to slave property and guaranteed the institution's protection in any territories the new nation might acquire. The "cornerstone" of the Confederacy, announced Davis's vice president, Alexander H. Stephens of Georgia, was "the great truth that the negro is not equal to the white man, that slavery, subordination to the superior race, is his natural and normal condition."

Even after rejecting the Crittenden Compromise, Lincoln by no means believed war inevitable. When he assumed office in March, eight slave states of the Upper South remained in the Union. Slaves and slaveholders in these states composed a considerably lower proportion of the population than in the Deep South, and large segments of the white population did not believe Lincoln's election justified dissolving the Union, even though virtually all Southern leaders accepted the *right* of a state to secede. Even within the Confederacy whites had divided over secession, with considerable numbers of nonslaveholding yeomen in opposition. In time, Lincoln believed, secession might collapse from within.

Thus, in his first month as President, Lincoln walked a tightrope—avoiding any action that might drive more states from the Union, encouraging Southern Unionists to assert themselves within the Confederacy, while at the same time seeking to quiet a growing clamor in the North for forceful action against secession. With the risk of war ever present, Lincoln strove to ensure that if hostilities did break out, the South would fire the first shot and bear the blame in Northern eyes. And that is precisely what happened on April 12, 1861, at Fort Sumter, an enclave of Union control in Charleston harbor. A few days earlier Lincoln had notified South Carolina's governor that he intended to replenish the garrison's dwindling supplies. Viewing the fort's presence as an affront to Southern nationhood and perhaps hoping to force the wavering Upper South to join the Confederacy, Jefferson Davis ordered batteries to fire on the

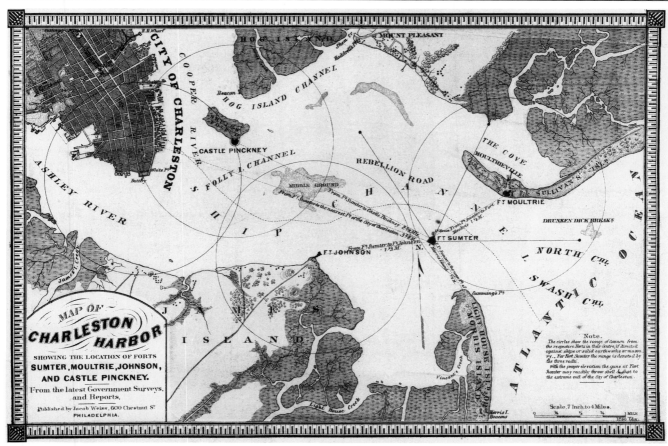

An 1861 map drawn by government surveyors shows the strategic importance of Fort Sumter, located at the entrance to Charleston harbor.

fort. On April 14 the garrison surrendered; the following day Lincoln proclaimed that an insurrection existed in the South and called for 75,000 troops to suppress it. Within weeks Virginia, North Carolina, Tennessee, and Arkansas, unwilling to supply soldiers to coerce sister slave states, joined the Confederacy. Civil war had begun.

"Both sides deprecated war," said Lincoln in his Second Inaugural, "but one of them would *make* war rather than let the nation survive; and the other would *accept* war rather than let it perish. And the war came."

Stephen A. Douglas in 1860.

STEPHEN ARNOLD DOUGLAS
(1813–1861)

Like Abraham Lincoln, Stephen A. Douglas moved west as a young man. Born and educated in Vermont, he settled first in New York State, then moved to Jacksonville, Illinois, in 1833. Admitted to the bar, he rose rapidly in Democratic party politics, serving on the state supreme court, in the legislature, and in Congress, and winning election to the U.S. Senate in 1847.

Douglas was the last great political leader to build a career on sectional compromise. It was he who shepherded the Compromise of 1850 through Congress. Douglas emerged during the critical years that followed as the nation's most powerful statesman. Popular sovereignty, the principle with which Douglas's career became identified, sought to remove the slavery issue from national politics. Only this, he believed, would keep sectional antagonism from destroying the Democratic party and the Union, while encouraging the development of the West. Douglas's failure to reach the presidency, or hold the Democratic party together, indicated that sectional compromise was no longer possible.

During the secession crisis, Douglas warned Southerners that Northern Democrats would stand with the federal government in the event of war. He died in June 1861.

A lithograph depicting Stephen A. Douglas as a champion of "popular sovereignty" and opponent of the proslavery Lecompton Constitution of Kansas.

The Battle of Gettysburg, *a lithograph by William C. Robertson, conveys the scope and drama of the Civil War's greatest battle.*

FIVE

THE FIRST MODERN WAR

The American Civil War is often called the first modern war. Never before had mass armies confronted each other on the battlefield with the deadly weapons created by the industrial revolution. The resulting casualties dwarfed anything in the American experience. The conflict did not begin as a total war, but it soon became that: a struggle that pitted society against society, in which the distinction between military and civilian targets all but disappeared. In a war of this kind the effectiveness of political leadership, the ability to mobilize economic resources, and a society's will to keep up the fight are as crucial to the final outcome as success or failure in individual battles.

Almost any comparison between the combatants seemed to favor the Union. The population of the North and loyal border slave states numbered 22 million, while only 9 million persons lived in the Confederacy, 3.5 million of them slaves. In manufacturing, railroad mileage, and financial resources—the sinews of modern war—the Union far outstripped the Confederacy. In 1860 New England manufactured over $2 million worth of firearms, sixty times as much as the entire South.

Nonetheless, the task confronting the Union also eclipsed that of the Confederacy. To win, the North had to conquer an area as large as Western Europe—a feat that had never been accomplished in modern times. The South had the advantage of fighting on its own soil, and more important, it did not have to conquer the North. Like George Washington's forces during the American Revolution, the South could lose most of the battles and still win the war, so long as it kept armies in the field and its opponent became convinced that victory was too costly. The South also had King Cotton on its side. The threat

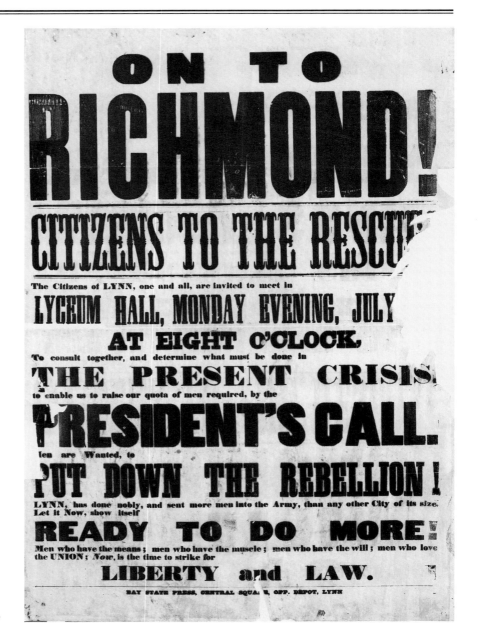

U.S. Army recruitment posters from 1861.

the war posed to the availability of cotton, Confederates believed, would soon lead the British and French to intervene on their side. No one knew at the outset that the South's faith in King Cotton would turn out to be misplaced. The large crops of 1859 and 1860 had created a huge stockpile in English warehouses. By the time distress hit the textile manufacturing districts in 1862, the government of Prime Minister Palmerston had decided not to intervene,

partly because Britain needed Northern wheat almost as much as Southern cotton.

The outbreak of war stirred powerful feelings of patriotism on both sides. Within days of the firing on Fort Sumter, tens of thousands of recruits, expecting a short, glorious war, heeded the call of the Union and the Confederacy. The formation of army units was organized at the local level, with leading citizens

Recruiting in the Park, *from* Harper's Weekly, *September 7, 1861, depicts the war's early days, when the Union Army relied entirely on volunteers to fill its ranks.*

creating companies and organizing recruitment drives. Later, as enthusiasm for enlistment waned, both sides resorted to conscription. The Confederacy in the spring of 1862 passed the first draft law in American history. Gradually extended as the war went on, the draft eventually covered all white men between the ages of seventeen and fifty, with exemptions for conscientious objectors, workers in such critical occupations as mining and railroads, and, most controversially, one adult male for every twenty slaves on a plantation. The North soon followed with its own draft law. On both sides, men wealthy enough to pay a prescribed amount of money or provide a substitute could escape military service.

All told, about 2.1 million men served in the Union Army, and 900,000 in the Confederate. Each army was a cross-section of its society—the North's composed largely of farm boys, artisans, and urban workers, the South's mostly of small farmers, with slaveholders dominating the officer corps. Beginning late in 1862, and accelerating after the Emancipation Proclamation, the North also recruited black soldiers into its forces, in segregated units with white commanders. By the end of the war some 190,000 black men had served in the Union Army and Navy. Although the Northern states enrolled free blacks from 1863 to the end of the war, the large majority of those who served were former slaves. Most hailed from the Mississippi Valley, where General Lorenzo Thomas actively recruited blacks from the plantations, and the loyal border states ex-

An 1861 lithograph, Departure of the 7th Regiment, *captures the exuberant spirit of the early days of the war.*

Colonel James A. Mulligan of Chicago, who organized the 23rd Illinois Volunteer Regiment, better known as the Irish Brigade, in 1861.

cluded from the Emancipation Proclamation, where military service remained for most of the war the only legal route out of slavery. In Kentucky, nearly sixty percent of adult black males entered the army; for the nation as a whole, over one-fifth of eligible blacks enlisted.

Within the army, blacks were anything but equal to whites. Black enlistment was initially intended to free whites for combat; accordingly, black recruits received lower pay and were mainly assigned to fatigue duty, construction work, and menial labor. Even after proving themselves in battle, they could not advance into the ranks of commissioned officers until 1865. If captured by Confederate forces they faced the prospect of summary execution (as happened to several dozen captured black soldiers at the Fort Pillow Massacre of 1864) or sale into slavery. Nonetheless, by proving themselves in battle and playing a central role in winning the war, black soldiers staked a claim to equal rights in the postwar republic. "Once let the black man get upon his person the brass letters U.S.," wrote Frederick Douglass, "and there is no power on earth which can deny that he has earned the right to citizenship."

Few of these recruits, white or black, had any military experience. Fifteen years had passed since the Mexican War, and even those who had served in state militias had learned little more than how to parade on holidays. Ideas about war were highly romantic—the stuff of novels, magazine articles, and lithographs. One private wrote home in 1862 that his notion of combat had come from "the pictures of battles he had seen . . . they would all be in a line, all standing in a nice level field fighting, a number of ladies taking care of the

Members of Battery A., 2d U.S. Colored Artillery, who fought at the Battle of Nashville, December 15–16, 1864. Blacks served in segregated units during the Civil War.

wounded, etc. But it isn't so." Nor were the recruits ready for military regimentation—"it comes rather hard at first to be deprived of liberty," wrote an Illinois recruit—or the monotony of life in camp. The constant round of drilling, ditch digging, and other chores was only occasionally interrupted by fierce bursts of fighting on the battlefield. In the first part of the war, the armies engaged in combat only sporadically, retiring to lick their wounds after battles and settling into semipermanent camps in winter to await the spring thaw. According to one estimate, during the first two years of the war the main Northern force, the Army of the Potomac, spent only thirty days in actual combat.

Neither the soldiers nor their officers were prepared for the way technology had transformed the nature of warfare. The Civil War was the first in which the railroad transported troops and supplies and the first to see railroad junctions (such as Chattanooga, Atlanta, and Petersburg) become major military objectives. It was the first to demonstrate the superiority of ironclads over wooden ships, thus revolutionizing naval warfare; the first in which balloons observed the enemy's lines, and the telegraph made possible instantaneous communication between generals. The war saw the introduction of armored trains, hand grenades, and even primitive submarines.

Perhaps most important, a revolution in arms manufacturing had replaced the traditional musket, accurate at only a short range, with the more modern rifle, easier to load and deadly at 600 yards or more because of its grooved (or "rifled") barrel. This development changed the nature of combat, emphasizing the importance of heavy fortifications and elaborate trenches and giving those on the defensive—usually the Southern armies—an immense advantage over those on the offensive. "My men," said Confederate General Thomas "Stonewall"

Colonel Elmer Ellsworth, head of the Chicago Zouave Cadets, photographed by Matthew Brady in 1860. Killed in 1861 while trying to capture a Confederate flag in Alexandria, Virginia, Ellsworth became the first Northern hero of the Civil War.

The sack coat worn by Union Army foot soldiers and the shell jacket worn by artillery men had simple designs based on standardized patterns that allowed the army and private contractors to produce them in great quantities.

Above right: The family of a German officer visited him at Hunter's Chapel, Virginia.
Right: A camp scene showing federal troops positioned along a railroad supply line.
Below: The Army of the Potomac photographed in camp in Virginia in May 1862.

Above: A carte de visite *of two unknown Union soldiers. These small, inexpensive photographs were produced by the thousands during the Civil War.*
Top: The 6th Regiment Vermont Volunteers, 1862.
Left: Sailors aboard an ironclad vessel in 1864.

Descriptive Roll of Company B

The Descriptive Roll of Company B, Illinois Volunteers, 1st Regiment, U.S. Light Artillery, lists the name, physical description, and history of every soldier in the unit, which saw major action at Fort Donelson in 1862 and the siege of Vicksburg in 1863.

First Regiment, U. S. Artillery Illinois Volunteers

ENLISTMENT				REMARKS
WHEN.	WHERE.	BY WHOM.	TERM.	
June 16	Cairo	Capt Taylor	The war	Discharged Jany 30th 1862 to enter the Gun Boat service
"	"	"	"	Promoted to Hospital Steward of the 1st Reg't Ills Lt. Artillery. July 6th 1863.
July 21	Chicago	"	"	Promoted to Corporal April 1st 1862 Promoted to Serg. Aug. 15. 1863
"	"	"	"	" " " Feby 1st 63 Promoted to 1st Corp. Aug. 15. 1863
"	"	"	"	Killed in action at Vicksburg. Miss. May 22d 63.
"	"	"	"	Promoted to Corp c/c. March 5, 465-1
" 22	"	"	"	Promoted to Corporal Aug 15. 1863
" 23	"	"	"	Promoted to Corporal. Feby 1st 63. Promoted to Gunner March 1st 63. Promoted to Serg't Sept 11/63
"	"	"	"	
"	"	"	"	
"	"	"	"	Promoted to Corporal c/c. Sept. 11/63
" 24	"	"	"	
"	"	"	"	Discharged for physical disability July 7th 1863
" 25	"	"	"	
"	"	"	"	Promoted to 1st Sergeant April 15th 1862 Promoted to Jr 1st Lt. Aug. 15th 1863
"	"	"	"	Died in St. Louis Hospital of Typhoid Fever. May 1st 1863
" 26	"	"	"	Discharged for physical disability & final statement given October 31st 1863.
"	"	"	"	Discharged pl O.F.S. Dec. 11. 63 Of War Dept. for promotion
"	"	"	"	Promoted to Corporal November 1st 1863. Promoted to Corp. Gunner Jan. 1 63.
"	"	"	"	
"	"	"	"	
"	"	"	"	Discharged for physical disability August 25th 1862.
"	"	"	"	Deserted from Camp at Memphis. Tenn October 26th 1862
"	"	"	"	
" 27	"	"	"	
"	"	"	"	Discharged for promotion November 12th 1862.
" 28	"	"	"	Discharged for promotion March 26th 1862
Aug 6	Birds Point	"	"	Promoted to Corporal Aug 1st 62. Reduced to the ranks at his own request Apr 1. 63.
July 31	Chicago	"	"	Discharged at Bridgeport Ala. by orders Adin Dept. of army of the Tenn. Nov. 18. 1863.
" 18	Birds Point	"	"	Deserted August 15th 1862. at Memphis. Tenn.
" 24	Birds Point	"	"	Discharged for Disability Dec 26th 1861 by order of Maj Gen'l Halleck
" 24	"	"	"	
Aug 16	"	"	"	Discharged for Disability May 5th 1863 & final statement given.
" 17	"	"	"	
" 24	Chicago	"	"	
" 22	"	"	"	Died Nov. 23 1863 from disease. at Gen'l Hospital 18th A.C. Bridgeport Ala.
"	"	"	"	
" 27	"	"	"	

Union Army camp equipment.

*Cards, dice, dominoes, and a gameboard
used by Civil War soldiers.*

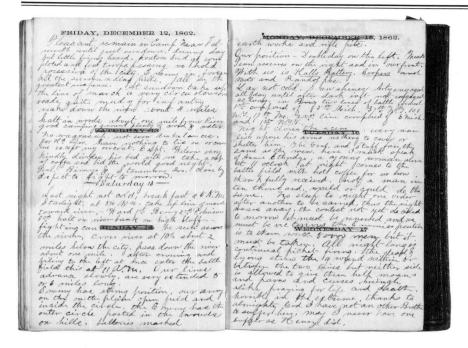

In 1862 Sergeant Silas S. Huntley of New York recorded his wartime experiences in this diary; the entry for December 12–13 describes the Battle of Fredericksburg.

[Handwritten margin notes:]

- Hospital Sketches
  ↓
  Identity - women - pre-civil war- confined to domestic role
  ↓
  transformed w/ civil war - most casualties of any war
  women became empowered
  ↓
  Men needing women
- MATERNAL

RACE REPRESENTATION
  ↓
  little black boy
  ↓
  cute line little baby to her → teaa to other nurses

→ goats, geese, colored people, coal
  ↓
  inanimate objects

Death + Dying
  ↓
  embrace death
  ↓
  death as relief from suffering

Jackson, "sometimes fail to drive the enemy from his position, but to hold one, never." The rifle reduced the effectiveness of cavalry charges and made hand-to-hand combat rare and bayonet wounds almost unheard of. The war of rifle and trench produced the appalling casualty statistics of Civil War battles. At Gettysburg there were 50,000 dead, wounded, and missing. All told, some 650,000 men died in the war (the equivalent, in terms of today's population, of more than 5 million deaths). Total casualties numbered well over 1 million. The death toll in the Civil War nearly equals the number of Americans who died in all the nation's other wars, from the Revolution to Vietnam.

Nor was either side prepared for other aspects of modern warfare. Both entered combat with no experience in dealing with large numbers of battlefield casualties. Medical care was primitve; for most wounds, amputation was almost automatic, with whiskey or a bullet held between the teeth as the only painkillers. "I believe the doctors kill more than they cure," wrote an Alabama private in 1862. Many more men perished from inadequate treatment of wounds and from diseases like measles, dysentery, malaria, and typhoid that swept through army camps, than died on the battlefield. (For black soldiers, especially the former slaves who entered the army in poorer health than whites, the death toll from disease was especially high.) The Civil War was also the first war in which large numbers of Americans were held in military prisons: 50,000 men died in these prisons, among them 13,000 Union soldiers at Andersonville in southwestern Georgia, victims of overcrowding, food shortages, and disease.

Another modern feature of the Civil War is that its brutal realities were

U.S. Infantry drum from the 9th Regiment of Vermont.

Soldiers traded coupons for goods at the sutler's tent, which sold tobacco and other provisions.

brought home with unprecedented immediacy to the public at large, especially in the North. Newspapers reported the results of battles on the following day and quickly published long lists of casualties. Via mass-produced images of camp and battle scenes, especially the ubiquitous three-dimensional stereograph, the infant art of photography carried the experience of modern war into millions of American homes. The technology was such that the camera could reproduce only static scenes—portraits of soldiers, camp life, preparations for battle, and the aftermath of conflict. For the "action" itself, the home front depended on artists who traveled with the armies and whose sketches were reproduced in illustrated magazines and individual lithographs.

But it was the photograph that, as the New York *Times* put it, became "the Clio of the war." When they went off to fight, thousands of soldiers posed for *cartes de visite*, small portraits mounted on cards, treasured by loved ones. Initially, photographs of the war itself showed few signs of bloodshed; in a sense they conformed to the romantic image of war widespread in both societies. But beginning in 1862, when photographers entered the battlefield to take shocking pictures of the dead lying in the fields of Antietam, the horror of modern war became tangible. The camera, in the words of one journalist, had "brought the bodies and laid them at our door-yards." "Let him who wishes to know what war is," wrote Oliver Wendell Holmes, "look at this series of illustrations." Holmes also noted that as a result of the war, photography had become "a vast branch of commerce." For men like Matthew Brady, an entrepreneur who organized a corps of photographers to cover the war, the conflict was a passport

Confederate dead at Antietam, as photographed by Alexander Gardner.

to notoriety and wealth. For photography itself, it was a turning point in public awareness and acceptance.

The outbreak of the war found both sides unprepared, although the North suffered more from the prevailing disorganization, since its task was so much greater. In 1861 there was no national banking system, no national railroad gauge, no tax system capable of raising the enormous funds needed to finance the war, not even accurate maps of the Southern states. Soon after the firing on Fort Sumter, Lincoln proclaimed a naval blockade of the South, but this was a purely theoretical gesture at a time when the navy required to patrol the South's 3,500-mile coastline consisted of ninety vessels, fewer than half of them steam-powered. Not until late in the war did the blockade become effective; until then, blockade running was a lucrative and not particularly dangerous way for enterprising men to serve the Southern cause and turn a handsome profit.

Problems of logistics and supply loomed as large for military planners as

Attack on Fort Wagner by artist and cartoonist Thomas Nast, illustrates both the bravery of black troops from the 54th Massachusetts Regiment and how popular racial imagery began to change as a result of black military service.

Tintype portraits of unidentified black Civil War soldiers, including a sergeant (with three stripes).

General Grant at Fort Donelson, *by French genre painter Paul D. Philippoteaux, depicts Grant on horseback (center) watching his troops advance on Fort Donelson, while the wounded receive treatment behind the lines.*

actual combat. The need for effective organization was especially acute for the Union, since as its armies penetrated the South, their lengthening supply lines required endless numbers of wagons, mules, horses, and railroad cars—inviting targets for Confederate raiders. Except in unusual circumstances when Union armies lived off the Southern countryside, such as during Grant's Vicksburg campaign and Sherman's March to the Sea, the task of guarding supply lines occupied an increasing percentage of Union troops. In the 1864 campaign for Atlanta, the number of men guarding the rail link back to Tennessee and Kentucky nearly equaled that of soldiers on the front line.

Both sides faced the daunting problem of purchasing and distributing the food and the millions of uniforms, shoes, blankets, tents, and other supplies required by the soldiers. With its greater industrial base and superior transportation system, the North solved the problem of supply more effectively than the South. Union soldiers never wanted for arms or other equipment. The Commissary Department drew upon the North's vast agricultural base to provide

General "Fighting Joe" Hooker (seated center) and his staff, photographed in June 1863, shortly before the Battle of Gettysburg.

General George B. McClellan, photographed in 1861.

soldiers with a plentiful if unexciting diet of bacon, beans, biscuits, and coffee, while Quartermaster General Montgomery C. Meigs dispensed over $1.5 billion for other supplies. Thanks to the successful mobilization of Northern resources, the Union Army became the best fed and best supplied military force in history. By the war's third year, on the other hand, Southern armies were suffering from acute shortages of food, uniforms, and shoes. Yet the chief of the Confederacy's Ordnance Bureau, Josiah Gorgas (a transplanted Northerner), proved brilliantly resourceful in arming Southern troops. Under his direction the Confederate government imported large numbers of weapons from abroad and established arsenals of its own to turn out rifles, artillery, and ammunition. Even when they were ill fed and ill clothed, Southern soldiers rarely lacked for arms.

Lincoln's early generals found it impossible to bring the Union's advantages in manpower, technology, and supply to bear on the battlefield. In April 1861 the regular army numbered little over 15,000 men, most of whom were stationed west of the Mississippi River. Its officers had no general staff and no strategic plans and were trapped in an older conception of warfare as a genteel pursuit carried on by small, professional armies. Few had ever seen armies as large as those that assembled in the early days of the war, and none relished the idea of leading totally untrained men into battle. Throughout the war, many men on both sides received commissions or promotions for political reasons or to balance ethnic and state representation. (Even Grant was initially commissioned through the influence of his friend, Congressman Elihu B. Washburne of Illinois.) The North also suffered from narrowness of military vision. Most of its generals initially

Photograph of General Robert E. Lee taken in Richmond.

The 1st Connecticut Artillery at Fort Richardson, Virginia, photographed in 1861.

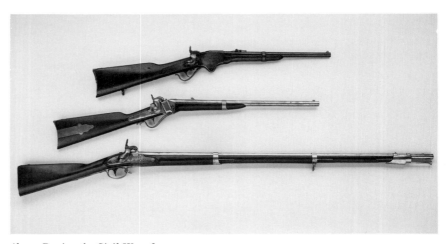

Above: During the Civil War, firearms manufacturers adapted older weapons and introduced new technology as illustrated by the Harper's Ferry musket (bottom), converted from the flintlock to the percussion system; the Sharps carbine (middle), employing a breech-loading mechanism; and the Spencer repeating carbine (top), which could fire seven cartridges in rapid succession.

Right: Cartridge box, tubes, and cartridges for the Spencer repeating carbine.

The Manhatten .36 caliber percussion revolver (top) and the Remington .44 caliber percussion revolver (bottom) were two of the most typical handguns carried by enlisted men.

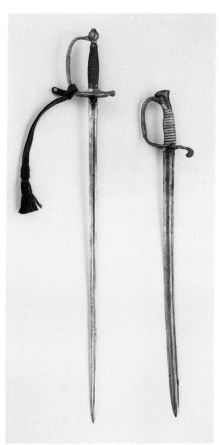

Two types of swords carried in the Civil War: Confederate officer's sword (right); Army regulation sword for noncommissioned officers (left).

Smoothbore howitzers were used in mountainous terrain or in the open field. The carriage broke down for transport by mule.

This hand-carved walnut gangway board, one of a pair, was used on the U.S.S. Hartford during the war.

concentrated on occupying Southern territory and attempting to capture Richmond, the Confederate capital. They attacked sporadically and withdrew after a battle, thus mitigating the North's manpower superiority and allowing the South to concentrate its smaller forces when an engagement impended.

Well before his generals, Lincoln realized that the South's armies, not its capital, had to be the North's objective. The president bitterly lamented his generals' failure to give chase and finish off the enemy after Union victories such as Antietam and Gettysburg. Lincoln, however, failed to realize that after major battles the number of casualties and general disorganization made pursuit almost impossible. Indeed, neither army was ever strong enough to annihilate the other, and in virtually every battle of the war the defeated side found safety in retreat. Thus, in a sense, the war could not truly be won on the battlefield. Few Americans realized at the outset that the conflict would continue until the South's ability and willingness to fight had been undermined, and slavery—the foundation of its economy—destroyed.

Not until 1864, when Ulysses S. Grant assumed command of all the Northern armies, did the Union effectively coordinate military activities in the war's different theaters. (The Confederacy never achieved this kind of modern command system, partly because Robert E. Lee, a brilliant battlefield tactician, lacked strategic vision and always considered the Virginia theater the South's paramount concern.) Until 1864 the Union's Eastern and Western operations were conducted

A battle flag from the 6th Virginia Cavalry displays the St. Andrew's Cross, the symbol most commonly used on Confederate battle flags.

Chicago Zouaves Cadets Drill Team Utica, New York, *painted by J. Graff, c. 1860, includes members of a Chicago unit (center), a New York unit (rear), and the Utica brass band (foreground). Organized by Elmer Ellsworth in Chicago in 1859, the Zouaves copied their colorful dress and precision drill after the French Zouaves of the Crimean War.*

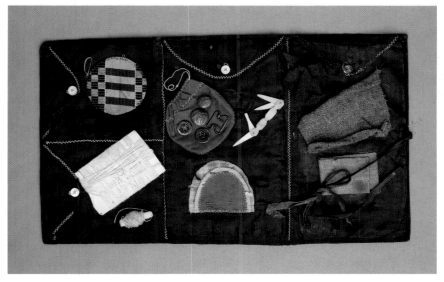

During the war soldiers carried a sewing kit known as a "housewife" for mending clothes. This kit, used by a volunteer from New Hampshire, contained needles, thread, buttons, and small pieces of extra material.

COME AND JOIN US BROTHERS.
PUBLISHED BY THE SUPERVISORY COMMITTEE FOR RECRUITING COLORED REGIMENTS
1210 CHESTNUT ST. PHILADELPHIA.

*A recruitment poster for black troops. Some
180,000 black soldiers served in the Union
Army.*

J. Joffray, a naive artist, recorded the capture of New Orleans, one of the Civil War's most significant Union victories, in Farragut's Fleet Passing Fort Jackson and Fort St. Philip, Louisiana, April 24, 1862.

Items such as this doll and potholders were sold at Chicago's Sanitary Fair in 1865 to raise money for soldiers and their families.

Women on the home front in Richmond made a Confederate flag of paper roses to support the war effort.

The Evacuation of Richmond, Va., *by Currier and Ives, dramatically depicts the last days of the war, when retreating Southern troops set fire to the Confedeate capital and thousands of its citizens fled before the advancing Union Army.*

Lincoln's Drive Through Richmond, *by
Dennis Malone Carter, depicts the president's
triumphal visit to the Confederate capital on
April 4, 1865.*

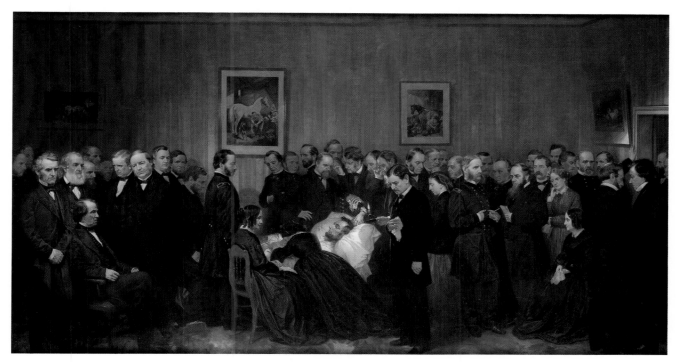

In The Death of Lincoln, *artist Alonzo Chappel gathers into one scene all those who visited the dying president throughout the night of April 14–15. Among the forty-seven people depicted are Mary and Robert Todd Lincoln, Andrew Johnson, Charles Sumner, and Edwin M. Stanton.*

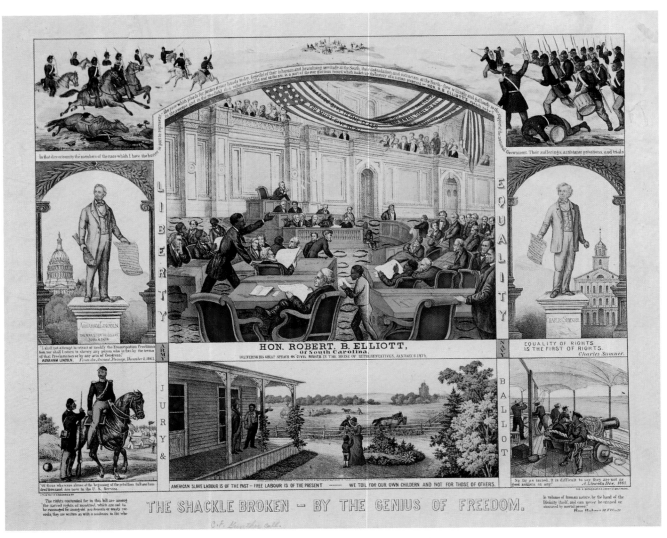

A lithograph from 1874 depicting momentous events of black history in the Civil War era, including emancipation, military service, and the advent of blacks in Congress, in this case South Carolina Representative Robert B. Elliott delivering a celebrated address in favor of the Civil Rights bill.

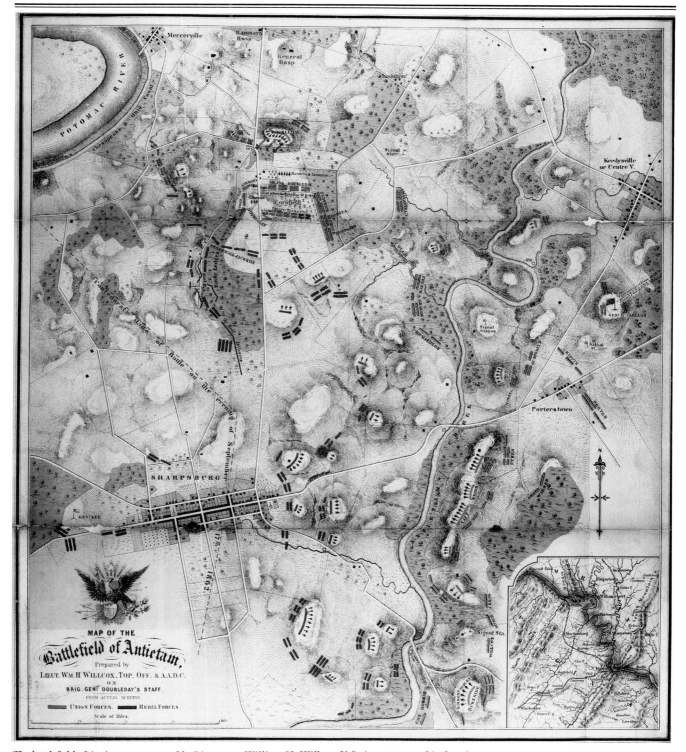

The battlefield of Antietam as mapped by Lieutenant William H. Willcox, U.S. Army topographical engineer.

Currier and Ives attempted to capture the fierceness of the fighting at the Battle of Antietam, September 17, 1862.

almost independently. In the East, most of the war's fighting took place in a narrow corridor between Washington and Richmond—a distance of only 120 miles—as a succession of Union generals led the Army of the Potomac toward the Confederate capital, only to be turned back by Southern forces. The war's first significant engagement, the first battle of Bull Run, took place on July 21, 1861, and ended with the chaotic retreat of the ill-trained Union soldiers back toward Washington. The equally disorganized Confederates were in no position to pursue them. Eight hundred men died at Bull Run, a toll eclipsed many times in the years to come, but still more than in any previous American battle. Though the encounter was strategically insignificant, it helped free both sides from the idea that the war would be a brief lark.

In the wake of Bull Run, both sides struggled to improve their organization and training. George B. McClellan, an army engineer who before the war had served as vice president of the Illinois Central Railroad and who had recently won a minor engagement with Confederate troops in western Virginia, assumed command of the Army of the Potomac. A brilliant organizer, McClellan succeeded in welding a superb fighting force. He seemed reluctant, however, to commit his men to battle. Whether this stemmed from McClellan's tendency to overestimate the size of the enemy or his hope that compromise might end the war without large-scale loss of life, the result was a prolonged period of inactivity in the East. Only in the spring of 1862, after a growing clamor for action by Republican newspapers, members of Congress, and an increasingly impatient Lincoln, did McClellan lead his army of over 100,000 men into Virginia. Here they confronted the smaller Army of Northern Virginia under the command of Robert E. Lee. The Seven Days' Campaign, a series of engagements on the peninsula south of Richmond, ended with the defeat of McClellan's forces and their withdrawal back to the vicinity of Washington. In August 1862, Lee again emerged victorious at the second battle of Bull Run against Union forces under the command of General John Pope.

Successful on the defensive, Lee now launched an invasion of the North, hoping to bring the border slave states into the Confederacy, induce Britain and France to recognize Southern independence, influence the North's fall elections, and perhaps capture Washington. At the battle of Antietam, in Maryland, McClellan and the Army of the Potomac repelled Lee's advance. In one day of fighting, nearly 6,000 men were killed and 17,000 wounded, a toll four times the American losses on D-day in World War II. The dead, one survivor recalled, lay three deep in the field, mowed down "like grass before the scythe." September 17, 1862, when the battle of Antietam was fought, remains the bloodiest day in all of American history.

Since Lee was forced to retreat, the North could claim Antietam as a victory, but it was to be the Union's last success in the East for some time. In December 1862 General Ambrose E. Burnside, who had replaced McClellan, launched a foolhardy and disastrous assault on Lee's army, entrenched on heights near Fredericksburg, Virginia. "It was not a fight," wrote one Union soldier to his mother, "it was a massacre." Burnside's troops suffered 12,600 casualties, more than twice Lee's losses. The following spring Lee defeated a Union army at Chancellorsville, although he lost his ablest lieutenant, "Stonewall" Jackson, mistakenly killed by fire from his own soldiers.

Lee now gambled on another invasion of the North, although his strategic objective remains unclear. Perhaps he believed a defeat on its own territory would destroy the morale of the Northern army and public. Perhaps he simply decided it was foolish to stay put while a succession of Northern generals launched attacks on his forces. In any case the two armies, with Union soldiers now under the command of General George G. Meade, met at Gettysburg, Pennsylvania, on the first three days of July 1863. With 165,000 troops involved, Gettysburg remains the largest battle ever fought on the North American continent. Lee found himself in the unaccustomed position of confronting entrenched Union forces, and against the advice of General James Longstreet, he decided to attack. The fighting culminated on July 3 with an assault on the Union center by Major General George E. Pickett's crack division. Withering artillery and rifle fire met the charge, and most of Pickett's troops never even reached the Union lines. Of the 14,000 men who made the advance—the flower of Lee's army—fewer than half returned. Later remembered as "the high tide of the Confederacy," Pickett's charge was also Lee's greatest blunder. His army retreated to Virginia, never again to set foot on Northern soil.

While the Union accomplished little in the East during the first two years of the war, except to repel Lee's two invasions of the North, events in the West followed a different course. Grant won the Union's first significant victory in February 1862, when he captured Forts Henry and Donelson on the Tennessee and Cumberland rivers in Tennessee. These successes opened a considerable part of the Confederate heartland to Union penetration. In April, naval forces under Admiral David G. Farragut occupied New Orleans, the South's largest city and the gateway to the Mississippi River, and the Union took control of the rich sugar plantation parishes to the city's south and west. At the same time Grant withstood a surprise Confederate attack at Shiloh. With over 20,000 killed and wounded, losses shared equally by the opposing armies, Shiloh was the first battle to produce the appalling casualties that soon became commonplace. After the first day of fighting, thousands lay unattended where they had fallen, and not even a raging thunderstorm could drown out the rasping of saws as surgeons amputated limbs from wounded men. "This night of horrors," wrote a Confederate survivor, "will haunt me to my grave."

A surgeon's kit used in the Civil War, containing amputation instruments, knives, and tourniquets, essential tools for wartime surgery.

Tents served as operating rooms in the field, as seen in this 1863 photograph. Unsanitary conditions and primitive medical methods resulted in a high death rate for both armies.

Photographs by Timothy O'Sullivan recorded the carnage of Gettysburg.

Libby Prison, a former warehouse on the James River in Richmond, housed more than 1,000 captured Union officers in unsanitary, crowded conditions.

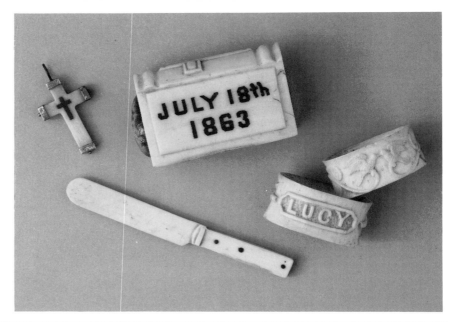

Colonel William H. Powell carved this pincushion, napkin rings, cross, and knife from animal bone while a federal prisoner in Richmond's Libby Prison.

Albert E. Myers, a Pennsylvania private stationed in Chicago, painted this view of Camp Douglas, a Union Army training post that served as a prison camp between 1862 and 1865. The prison held more than 30,000 Southern soldiers in harsh conditions.

Grant managed to retain control of the battlefield at Shiloh, but in the West, as in Virginia, the Union's advance soon lost momentum. Moving into Mississippi in November 1862, Grant unsuccessfully assaulted Vicksburg, from whose heights, defended by miles of trenches and earthworks, the Confederacy commanded the central Mississippi River. When direct attacks failed (as did an attempt to dig a canal that would divert the Mississippi, leaving Vicksburg high and dry), Grant devised a brilliant and audacious strategy. Moving his army south past the city, he cut himself off from his lines of supply and from communication with an anxious Lincoln, and launched a siege. Not until July 4, 1863, the same day that Lee began his retreat from Gettysburg, did Vicksburg surrender, and with it John C. Pemberton's army of 30,000 men—a loss the Confederacy could ill afford. The entire Mississippi Valley was now in Union

Confederate prisoners-of-war at Camp Douglas in 1864.

hands. The simultaneous defeats at Gettysburg and Vicksburg dealt a heavy blow to Southern morale. "Today absolute ruin seems our portion," Ordnance Chief Gorgas wrote in his diary. "The Confederacy totters to its destruction." But nearly two years were to pass before the Union's final victory.

Only in 1864, when Grant engaged in a long-term war of attrition against Lee's forces in Virginia and Sherman brought the wrath of his army to the heart of Georgia, did the North find generals attuned to the realities of modern war. Although both men had attended West Point, neither was cut from the mold of the professional officer, and both had long experience in civilian life. Sherman knew the South well, having served before the war as head of a military academy in Louisiana. Grant's logical, determined mind seemed to typify the industrial age. He was one of the few generals on either side who could visualize an entire battle as it occurred, even as reports poured in of individual engagements and troop movements. He understood that to bring the North's manpower advantage into play he must attack simultaneously and unremittingly "all along the line," thereby preventing the enemy from concentrating its forces or retreating to safety after an engagement. He was willing to accept the high casualties an army continuously on the offensive was bound to suffer, knowing that the North could replace its losses and the South could not. And both Grant and Sherman understood that no single battle would end the war. As Grant later wrote in his memoirs, he had been convinced ever since Shiloh that the Union could not be saved "except by complete conquest."

In May 1864 the Army of the Potomac crossed the Rapidan River to do battle with Lee's forces in Virginia. At the same time Sherman's forces moved from Union-controlled Tennessee into Georgia, threatening Atlanta. There followed a month of the war's bloodiest fighting. In the Battle of the Wilderness, Grant's 115,000-man army suffered 18,000 casualties, while Lee's far smaller forces suffered 7,500. Previous Union generals had broken off engagements after losses of this magnitude. But Grant continued to press forward, attacking again at Spotsylvania, and again at Cold Harbor, where he lost 7,000 men in a single hour. At the end of six weeks of fighting, Grant's casualties stood at 60,000—almost the size of Lee's entire army—while Lee had lost 25,000 men. With daily combat and a fearsome casualty toll, the fighting in Virginia was a turning point in modern warfare, a forerunner of the prolonged, sustained, and even bloodier actions of World War I.

Grant had become the only Union general to maintain the initiative against Lee in the Eastern theater, although at a cost that led critics to label the Union general a "butcher of men." But still victory eluded him. Finally, Lee's army retreated to Petersburg, and Grant settled in for a prolonged siege. Meanwhile the Union cavalry, led by General Philip H. Sheridan, rode through the Shenandoah Valley, Virginia's breadbasket, destroying everything in its path in an attempt to weaken Southern resolve and starve Lee's army into submission. So thorough were Sheridan's depredations, it was said, that a bird flying over the Valley would henceforth have to carry its own food.

Like Grant, Sherman encountered dogged resistance from Confederate forces. Not until September did he finally enter Atlanta. In November, Sherman and his army of 60,000 set out on the famous March to the Sea. Abandoning its supply lines and communications, the army lived off the land, while cutting a sixty-mile-wide swath of destruction through Georgia. Thousands of slaves abandoned the plantations to follow this avenging host, which destroyed railroads, buildings, and all the food and supplies it could not use. His aim, Sherman wrote, was "to make Georgia howl"—"to whip the rebels, to humble their pride, to follow them to their innermost recesses, and make them fear and dread us." Here was modern war in all its destructiveness, and even though few civilians were physically harmed, the March made Sherman's name a byword for cruelty among Southerners. Sherman had a ready answer to his critics: "War is cruelty and you cannot refine it. . . . If they want peace, they and their relatives must stop the war."

Three days before Christmas 1864, Sherman's army captured Savannah. With Lee bottled up at Petersburg and Union forces fully in control of the Western theater, Northern victory at last appeared inevitable, although at a cost no one in 1861 could have foreseen.

Whatever myths later generations invented, there was no romance in the Civil War. "You can form no idea of a battlefield," a soldier from Maine wrote

George Barnard served as official photographer for the Union Army in 1864–65 and accompanied General Sherman on his March to the Sea and subsequent foray into South Carolina. These vivid scenes show the Potter home in Atlanta (above) and the Charleston railroad depot (right).

home after Gettysburg. "No tongue can tell its horror. I hope none of my brothers will ever have to go into a fight." Yet an understanding of the brutal reality of modern war was not the only lasting result of the conflict. Unintended by either Lincoln or Davis, the Civil War unleashed forces that transformed both Northern and Southern societies and gave the nation a "new birth of freedom."

An unknown photographer recorded Walker the Artist at Work on Lookout Mountain *in November 1863. Publications like* Harper's Weekly *employed scores of artists to document the war. Their sketches were made into wood engravings and printed in newspapers.*

Photograph of General Ulysses S. Grant at his headquarters in City Point, Virginia, in 1864.

ULYSSES SIMPSON GRANT
(1822–1885)

"The art of war is simple enough. Find out where your enemy is. Get at him as soon as you can. Strike at him as hard as you can and as often as you can, and keep moving on." Ulysses S. Grant followed his own advice as he waged war for the Union Army between 1861 and 1865.

Nothing in Grant's early life seemed to mark him for greatness. He attended West Point but graduated in the lower half of his class. He left the army in 1854, and when war broke out was a clerk in a Galena, Illinois, leather goods store.

As one of the few residents of Illinois with military training, Grant received a commission as colonel of the 21st Illinois Volunteers. A series of victories in the West, notably at Forts Henry and Donelson in 1862 and Vicksburg and Chattanooga in 1863, led Lincoln to appoint him General-in-Chief of the Union Armies.

Unlike General George McClellan, Grant fully accepted the military's subordination to civilian leaders in matters of policy. After the Emancipation Proclamation he worked diligently to ensure blacks' freedom and to enlist black soldiers.

Beginning in May 1864, Grant initiated a campaign of continuous engagement with Lee's army in Virginia, culminating in the seige of Petersburg. Union troops suffered heavy casualties and critics attacked Grant as a "butcher." In April 1865 Grant forced Lee to surrender.

After the war, Grant served two terms as president and wrote an extremely popular volume of memoirs.

Grant used this black leather saddle during the Civil War. The embossed star on the stirrup hood designates the rank of general.

Emancipated Negroes Celebrating the Emancipation Proclamation of President Lincoln, *depicted in the French newspaper* Le Monde Illustré.

SIX

WAR, POLITICS,
AND SOCIETY

War, it has been said, is the midwife of revolution, and the Civil War produced far-reaching changes in American life. Most dramatic was the destruction of slavery, the central institution of Southern society. Even though the Lincoln administration at first insisted that slavery was irrelevant to the conflict, blacks saw the outbreak of fighting as heralding the long awaited end of their bondage. With this conviction, the slaves took actions that propelled a reluctant white America down the road to emancipation.

The disintegration of slavery began with the war itself. As the Union Army occupied territory on the periphery of the Confederacy and later in its heartland, slaves by the thousands abandoned plantations and headed for Union lines. (Not a few passed along valuable military intelligence concerning the deployment of Confederate troops and detailed knowledge of the South's terrain and roads.) Thousands of others remained at home but quickly grasped that the presence of occupying troops destroyed the coercive power of both individual masters and the slaveholding community. In southern Louisiana, for example, the arrival of the Union Army in 1862 led slaves to sack plantation houses and refuse to work unless wages were paid. Slavery there, wrote a Northern reporter in November 1862, "is forever destroyed and worthless, no matter what Mr. Lincoln or anyone else may say on the subject."

The determination of blacks to seize the opportunity presented by the war at first proved a burden to the army and an embarrassment to the president. Lincoln's paramount concern in the war's first year was to keep the slave states of Delaware, Maryland, Kentucky, and Missouri within the Union and to build the broadest base of support in the North for the war effort. Were the Union to

Photographs of "contrabands," or refugee slaves, in Union Army camps.

lose the border states, with their white population of 2.6 million and their half million slaves, "the job on our hands," Lincoln wrote, would be "too large for us." Action against slavery could drive these states into the Confederacy and alienate moderate and conservative Northerners. In 1861 the restoration of the Union, not emancipation, was the cause that generated broad public support. For this reason, in the early days of the war Congress adopted the Crittenden Resolution, affirming that the Union had no intention of interfering with slavery. Northern military commanders even returned fugitive slaves to their owners, a policy that raised an outcry in antislavery circles. Yet as the Confederacy set slaves to work as military laborers and the flight from the plantations accelerated, the policy of ignoring slavery unraveled. By the end of 1861 the military had adopted the plan, inaugurated in Virginia by General Benjamin F. Butler, of treating escaped blacks as "contraband of war"—that is, property of military value subject to confiscation—and employing them as laborers for the Union armies.

Meanwhile, the failure of traditional strategies to produce victory in 1861 and 1862 strengthened the hand of Northerners, including Radical Republicans and abolitionists, who insisted that emancipation was necessary to weaken the South's capacity to sustain its war effort. Their appeals won increasing support in a Congress frustrated by the lack of military success. In March 1862, Congress expressly prohibited the army from returning fugitive slaves. Then came abolition in the District of Columbia and the territories, followed by the Second Confiscation Act, which liberated slaves in Union-occupied territory if their masters were disloyal.

After futile pleas to the border states to free their slaves voluntarily and a flirtation with the idea of colonizing blacks outside the country, Lincoln in the summer of 1862 decided that emancipation had become a political and military necessity. But on the advice of Secretary of State William H. Seward he delayed announcement of the new policy until after a Northern victory, lest it seem an act of desperation. When McClellan's army forced Lee to retreat at Antietam, Lincoln took the opportunity to warn the South that unless it laid down its arms, he would decree abolition on January 1, 1863. On that day he signed the Emancipation Proclamation. Because its legality derived from the president's constitutional authority as military commander-in-chief, the proclamation applied to areas still in rebellion; it exempted slave regions under Union control, where, in effect, the war had ended—the loyal border states and areas of the Confederacy occupied by Union soldiers, such as Tennessee and southern Louisiana. But the vast majority of the South's slaves, well over 3 million men, women, and children, Lincoln decreed, "are and henceforth shall be free."

The Emancipation Proclamation profoundly altered the nature of the war and the future course of American history. Firing the Northern war effort with moral purpose, it transformed a war of armies into a conflict of societies, ensuring that Union victory would produce a social revolution within the South and a redefinition of the place of blacks in American life. Despite the fact that it only applied to territory outside the Union's control, it presaged complete abolition. For if slavery perished in Mississippi and South Carolina, it could hardly survive in Kentucky, Tennessee, and a few parishes of Louisiana. In his annual message to Congress in December 1861, Lincoln had assured the Northern public that

President Lincoln photographed on February 9, 1864, by Anthony Berger for the studio of Matthew Brady.

the war would "not degenerate into a violent and remorseless revolutionary struggle." With the Emancipation Proclamation, this was precisely what it had become.

The evolution of Lincoln's emancipation policy displayed the hallmark of his wartime leadership—a capacity for growth and the ability to elicit broad public support for his administration. Lincoln understood that the war had created a fluid situation that placed a premium on flexibility and made far-reaching change inevitable. But his step-by-step approach to emancipation made the measure more palatable to the border states and moderate Northerners, even though the Democratic opposition denounced the proclamation as a violation of the Constitution and a threat to white supremacy. Throughout the war, despite criticism from both Radical and moderate Republicans, Lincoln generally remained on good terms with his party's various factions. And despite the ebb and flow of public morale in the face of often discouraging news from the front, he remained able to inspire popular support for the war effort. In mobilizing public opinion, Lincoln was assisted by a vast propaganda effort comprising lithographs, souvenirs, sheet music, and the like issued by patriotic organizations and commercial enterprises, and a flood of tracts sponsored by the War Department. These pieces tarred the Democratic party with the brush of treason and accused the South of all manner of atrocities against Union soldiers and loyal civilians.

But it was Lincoln himself who linked the conflict with the deepest values of Northern society. At the outset he described the war as a struggle of worldwide significance that "presents to the whole family of man, the question, whether a constitutional republic, or a democracy" could survive. He drew upon the familiar free labor ideology to argue that only Union victory would guarantee Northerners continued opportunity to enjoy economic mobility and "an unfettered start, a fair chance, in the race of life." In his speech at the dedication of the Gettysburg cemetery in November 1863, Lincoln defined the very essence of democratic government: the sacrifices of Union soldiers would ensure that "government of the people, by the people, for the people, shall not perish from the earth."

Nonetheless, while invoking traditional values, Lincoln presided over profound changes in Northern life. The effort to mobilize the resources of the Union greatly enhanced the power of the federal government and of a rising class of

ABE LINCOLN'S LAST CARD OR, ROUGE-ET-NOIR.

Cartoonist John Tenniel satirized the Emancipation Proclamation for the English magazine Punch *as the last resort of a desperate gambler.*

On this mahogany table, Lincoln reportedly drafted the Emancipation Proclamation. The Gothic-style chair was used at the White House during the Lincoln presidency.

FILLING CARTRIDGES AT THE UNITED STATES ARSENAL, AT WATERTOWN, MASSACHUSETTS.—[SEE NEXT PAGE.]

This wood engraving from a sketch by Winslow Homer, from Harper's Weekly, *illustrates how women were drawn into factory labor in war-related industries.*

industrial entrepreneurs. Nourished by wartime inflation and government contracts, the profits of industry boomed. New England mills worked day and night
to supply the army with blankets and uniforms, while Pennsylvania coal mines
and ironworks rapidly expanded their production. Mechanization proceeded
apace in many industries, especially those like boot and shoe production and
meatpacking that supplied the army's ever increasing needs. Chicago, the country's railroad and slaughterhouse capital, experienced unprecedented growth in
population, construction, banking, and manufacturing. Agriculture also flourished, for even as farm boys by the hundreds of thousands joined the army,
the frontier of cultivation pushed westward, with machines and immigrant hands
replacing lost labor. Numerous Americans who would take the lead in reshaping
the nation's postwar economy created or consolidated their fortunes during the
Civil War, among them Andrew Carnegie, John D. Rockefeller, Jay Gould,
J. P. Morgan, and Philip D. Armour. These and other "captains of industry"
managed to escape military service, some by hiring substitutes.

At the same time, Congress adopted policies that promoted further economic
expansion and permanently altered the North's financial system. To encourage
agricultural development, the Homestead Act offered free public land to settlers
in the West. To further consolidate the Union, Congress made huge land grants
for internal improvements, especially the construction of a transcontinental
railroad, chartered in 1862. And to help finance the war the government raised
the tariff, imposed new taxes on production and consumption and license fees
on every profession but the ministry, and enacted the nation's first income tax,
a graduated levy that reached a maximum rate of ten percent. Moreover, it

*Among the patriotic items produced by
Northern manufacturers during the war were
this spittoon deriding the Confederate flag
and a pitcher commemorating the death of
Colonel Elmer Ellsworth.*

The bloody New York City draft riots of 1863 escalated from an attempt to block the implementation of the draft to a wholesale assault on the city's black population.

issued nearly $400 million in paper money (establishing the first national currency in American history), floated an enormous national debt, and established a national system of banks chartered by the federal government.

Like emancipation and conscription, these measures vastly increased the power and size of the federal government. The federal budget for 1865 exceeded $1 billion (twenty times the budget for 1860), and with its new army of clerks, tax collectors, and other officials, the federal government became the nation's largest employer. A British newspaper predicted in 1861 that the conflict would "draw together the Northern states as they have never been drawn before . . . and finally will impress them with the absolute necessity of a . . . stronger central power." Republicans exalted the government's continuing maturation as one of the most salutary of the war's consequences. "The policy of this country," declared Senator John Sherman of Ohio, "ought to be to make everything national as far as possible; to nationalize our country so that we shall love our country." The period's rising spirit of nationalism was expressed in the term now adopted by many Northerners to refer to the country itself: instead of a "union" of separate states, it had become a single, consolidated "nation."

Despite Lincoln's political sagacity, the war and his administration's policies produced deep divisions within Northern society. Republicans labeled those opposed to the war Copperheads, after a poisonous snake that strikes without warning. Strongest in the lower Northwest, with its large Southern-born population, and among working-class Catholic immigrants in Eastern cities, disaffection arose not only from war weariness produced by military defeats and mounting casualties but from the rapid changes the conflict produced in Northern life.

As the war progressed it heightened existing social tensions and created new ones. Northerners attuned to traditional notions of local autonomy feared the growing power of the federal government, especially since the administration, to quell dissent, suspended the writ of habeas corpus, arrested political opponents, and temporarily suppressed newspapers for articles critical of the war. Others resented the profits reaped by manufacturers and financiers, who spent money, one magazine reported, "with a profusion never before witnessed in our country," while workers saw their real incomes shrink because of inflation. Indeed, the war witnessed the rebirth of the Northern labor movement, which organized numerous strikes for higher wages. And the prospect of a sweeping change in the status of blacks called forth a racist reaction in many parts of the North. In July 1863 the introduction of conscription provoked the New York City draft riots, in which angry crowds assaulted the symbols of the new order being created by the war: draft offices, the mansions of wealthy Republicans, industrial establishments, and the city's black population. The riots became the most violent civil upheaval in American history except for the South's rebellion itself. For four days a mob controlled the nation's commercial capital, and only the arrival of troops fresh from the battlefields of Gettysburg quelled the uprising.

Opposition to the war, however, was generally expressed through the Democratic party, which subjected Lincoln's policies to withering criticism. The Democrats themselves remained divided between those who supported the military effort while criticizing policies like emancipation and the draft and others who favored immediate peace. Nonetheless, as war weariness mounted in 1864, exacerbated by Grant's appalling casualty tolls, Lincoln for a time believed he would be unable to win reelection. (No president had been reelected since Andrew Jackson in 1832, and none even renominated since Martin Van Buren in 1840.) To oppose Lincoln the Democrats chose General George B. McClellan, although his candidacy was compromised from the outset by a platform calling for an immediate armistice and peace conference—a plan that even war-weary Northerners viewed as tantamount to surrender. In the end, buoyed by Sherman's capture of Atlanta, which suggested that an end to the war was in sight, Lincoln won a sweeping victory, capturing fifty-five percent of the vote and

Thomas Nast produced this lithograph in honor of the U.S. Sanitary Commission, whose work aided soldiers at the front lines and in hospitals.

carrying every state but Kentucky, Delaware, and New Jersey. Three-quarters of the soldiers in the Union Army voted for Lincoln, an indication that they remained willing to prosecute the war until the Confederacy had been defeated.

If some Northerners resented the changes brought about by the war, others found that the conflict opened new doors of opportunity. Long excluded from public life, hundreds of thousands of women now took part in organizations that gathered medical and other supplies for soldiers and sent books, clothing, and food to the freedmen. Although at the highest levels control remained in male hands, these societies afforded women both independence and training in organization. Women played the leading role in the Sanitary Fairs—grand bazaars where military banners, uniforms, and other relics of the war were displayed and donated items sold to raise money for soldiers' aid. From the ranks of this wartime mobilization came many of the leaders of the postwar movement for women's rights. Women also took advantage of the wartime labor shortage to move into jobs in factories and into certain largely male professions. Many

MAIN BUILDING OF
THE GREAT NORTH WESTERN SANITARY FAIR
CHICAGO.
OPENED MAY 30 th 1865

The main building of the Great Northwest Sanitary Fair of 1865 stood at the corner of Randolph Street and Michigan Avenue in Dearborn Park, Chicago. In three weeks, the fair raised more than $300,000.

Like other women's groups during the war, The Soldiers' Aid Society of Springfield, Illinois, collected food and made clothing for the troops.

of these wartime gains proved temporary, but in nursing, white collar government jobs, and retail sales, women found a permanent place.

Social change and internal turmoil also engulfed much of the South. The destruction of slavery was only one facet of the transformation wrought by the war in Southern life. As in the North, women mobilized to support soldiers in the field and stepped out of traditional roles to manage farms and plantations, run commercial establishments, and work in arms factories. In Richmond, Southern "government girls" staffed many of the clerkships in the new Confederate bureaucracy.

Nonetheless, public disaffection became an even more serious problem for the Confederacy than it was for the Union. Even as it waged a desperate struggle for independence, the South was increasingly divided against itself. After an initial burst of patriotic enthusiasm, many nonslaveholders became convinced that they were bearing an unfair share of the war's burdens. In some small farming areas, such as east Tennessee, outright resistance to the Confederacy was widespread from the start. Southern authorities responded by imprisoning Unionists and seizing their property, and thousands escaped through the mountains to enlist in the Union Army. Elsewhere, disaffection developed more slowly. The draft, with its provision exempting one white male on every plantation of twenty slaves (thus releasing many overseers and planters' sons from service), convinced many yeomen that the struggle for Southern independence had become a "rich man's war and a poor man's fight."

As the blockade tightened, Union occupation spread, and production by slaves declined, disaffection also arose from shortages of such essential commodities as salt, corn, and meat. (Southerners displayed remarkable ingenuity in their attempts at inventing substitutes, such as "Confederate coffee," made from peas, corn, and okra, and "Confederate leather," a kind of cotton cloth.) Lying at the war's strategic crossroads, portions of the Southern upcountry were laid waste by the march of opposing armies. The devastation, which stood in glaring contrast to the North's economic boom, was an inevitable result of the war. But Confederate government policies exacerbated its effects. Like the Union, the Confederacy borrowed heavily to finance the war and issued paper money that produced rampant inflation. Unlike federal lawmakers, however, the planter-dominated Confederate Congress proved unwilling to levy heavy taxes that planters would have to pay. Instead it enacted a tax-in-kind (a levy of ten percent on agricultural produce) and authorized the practice of impressment, whereby military officers could seize farm goods to support the army. By the middle of the war, Lee's army relied largely on food impressed from farms and plantations in Georgia and South Carolina. These policies were deeply resented by small farmers for undermining their subsistence agriculture. "The Rebel army treated us a heap worse than Sherman did," a Georgia farmer later recalled. "I had hogs, and a mule, and a horse, and they took them all."

Jefferson Davis, the Confederacy's only president, in a portrait by Christian F. Schwerdt.

 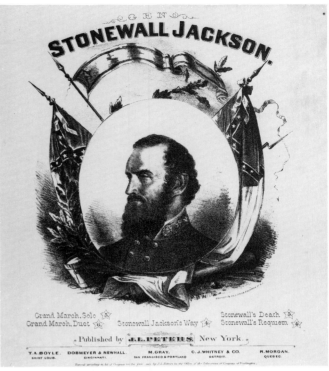

Patriotic sheet music of the Confederacy.

During the war, numerous yeoman families sank into poverty and debt. Food riots broke out in many places, including Richmond, where in 1863 a large crowd of women plundered army food stocks. They dispersed only when President Davis himself arrived on the scene and threatened to have troops open fire. By 1864 organized peace movements had appeared in several states, and secret societies such as the Heroes of America were actively promoting disaffection and assisting Southern Unionists to reach federal lines.

The man charged with the task of maintaining Southern unity and rallying public support for the Confederacy proved unequal to the task. Born, like Lincoln, to humble circumstances in Kentucky, Jefferson Davis had moved to Mississippi as a youth, attended West Point, and after his return home acquired a large plantation. Aloof, stubborn, and humorless, he lacked both Lincoln's common touch and his flexibility and proved far less successful at instilling a sense of common purpose in his people. Holding an exaggerated belief in his own military abilities, Davis fussed over minor army matters while devoting little attention to the deteriorating economic situation. Unlike Lincoln, who enlisted the Republican party's outstanding figures in his cabinet—men like Secretary of State Seward and Secretary of the Treasury Salmon P. Chase—Davis surrounded himself with figures of second rank who brought little substance to his administration. Nor did he deal effectively with obstructionist gov-

On April 2, 1863, food shortages and high prices led to widespread rioting by Richmond women, a sign of growing disaffection within the Confederacy.

ernors like Joseph E. Brown, who denounced the Confederate draft as "a dangerous usurpation . . . of the reserved rights of the states" and insisted that Georgia troops must be commanded by Georgia officers. So inferior to Lincoln was Davis as a wartime leader that one historian has suggested that if the North and South had exchanged presidents, the South would have won the war.

Joshua B. Moore, a slaveholder in northern Alabama, commented in 1862 on the social changes he was certain the war would produce: "There are but some or a little over 300,000 men taking all the slave states that are . . . owners of slaves. Now men who have no interest in it are not going to fight through a long war to save it—never. They will tire of it and quit." As the war progressed and disillusionment replaced initial enthusiasm, desertion became what one officer called a "crying evil" for the Southern armies. By the war's end over 100,000 men had deserted, almost all of them, a Southern leader observed, from among "the poorest class of nonslaveholders whose labor is indispensable to the daily support of their families." Men, another official noted, "cannot be expected to fight for the government that permits their wives and children to starve." The decline of home front morale and military discipline sapped the Confederacy's ability to conduct the war and hastened its final collapse. Internal dissent, wrote John A. Campbell, the South's assistant secretary of war, "menaces the existence of the Confederacy as fatally as . . . the armies of the United States."

The growing shortage of white manpower led Confederate authorities in March 1865 to launch a program no one could have foreseen when the war began: the arming of slaves to fight for the South. The war ended before the recruitment of blacks actually began, and it remains uncertain how many slaves would have been willing to fight alongside their masters. But the South's decision to raise black troops illustrates how the war not only undermined slavery but challenged the very essence of Southern ideology. "The day you make soldiers of them is the beginning of the end of the revolution," declared Howell Cobb, a Georgia planter and politician who had chaired the convention that created the Confederacy in February 1861. "If slaves make good soldiers, our whole theory of slavery is wrong."

After Lincoln's reelection, the war hastened to its conclusion. In January 1865 Sherman moved from Georgia into South Carolina, sowing even greater destruction and bringing, as one rice planter recorded in his journal the "breath of Emancipation." Anarchy reigned on the plantations as slaves drove off remaining overseers, destroyed planters' homes, plundered smokehouses and storerooms, and claimed the land for themselves. Meanwhile, on January 31, Congress approved the Thirteenth Amendment, which abolished slavery throughout the entire Union. (By this time, slavery existed legally only in Kentucky and Delaware, for Republican governments had come to power in Missouri, Maryland, Louisiana, and Tennessee and abolished the peculiar institution.)

On April 2 Grant finally broke through Lee's lines at Petersburg, forcing the Army of Northern Virginia to abandon the city and leaving Richmond defenseless. The following day, Union soldiers occupied the Southern capital, but not before fires set by retreating Confederates destroyed a large part of the city. Blacks thronged the streets, dancing, singing, and praying, exulting particularly at the sight of a unit of black soldiers. On April 4, heedless of his own safety, Lincoln walked the streets of Richmond accompanied only by a dozen sailors. At every step he was besieged by emancipated slaves who hailed him as a messiah. Lee and his army meanwhile headed west, only to be cut off and encircled by Grant. Realizing further resistance was useless, Lee surrendered

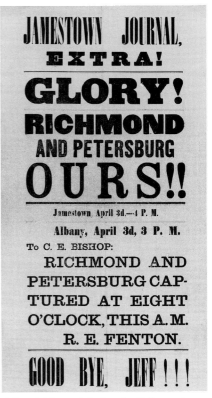

JAMESTOWN JOURNAL,
EXTRA!
GLORY!
RICHMOND
AND PETERSBURG
OURS!!

Jamestown, April 3d.—4 P. M.
Albany, April 3d, 3 P. M.
To C. E. BISHOP:
RICHMOND AND
PETERSBURG CAP-
TURED AT EIGHT
O'CLOCK, THIS A. M.
R. E. FENTON.

GOOD BYE, JEFF !!!

A broadside proclaiming the Union capture of Richmond and Petersburg. Within six days the war would be over.

Ruins in Richmond, 1865.

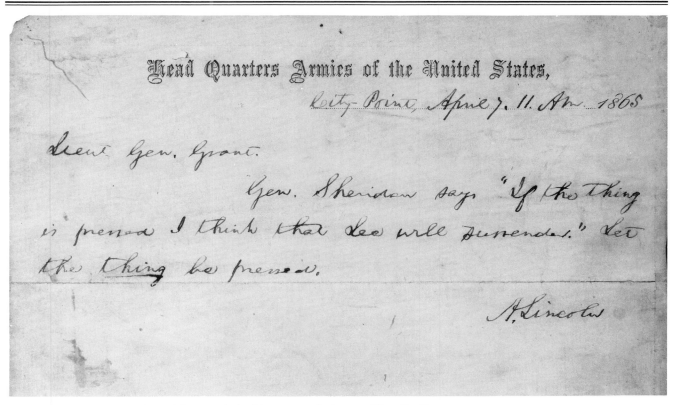

Lincoln's succinct message to General Grant, ordering him to pursue Lee's army: "Gen. Sheridan says 'If the thing be pressed I think that Lee will surrender.' Let the thing be pressed."

Upon this table from the McLean home at Appomattox Court House, Lee signed the terms of surrender that ended the Civil War. News of the surrender passed over this telegraph instrument from the town's railroad depot.

The Assassination of President Lincoln, *a
lithograph by Currier and Ives.*

at Appomattox Court House on April 9. Although some Confederate units
remained in the field, the Civil War was over.

Lincoln did not live to savor victory. On Good Friday, April 14, the president
was mortally wounded by the pro-Confederate actor John Wilkes Booth. Booth
and his coconspirators had earlier planned to kidnap Lincoln and spirit him to
Richmond; after Lee's surrender they determined to murder the president along
with high-ranking members of the administration. Lincoln died the next day,
mourned by whites as the man who had saved the Union and freed the slaves,
and by blacks as a divinely appointed savior. His body was carried by train to
its Illinois resting place on a circuitous 1,600-mile journey that illustrated how
tightly the railroad now bound the Northern states. But events along the way
hinted at problems to come. When the train reached New York City, municipal
authorities tried to bar blacks from marching in the memorial procession, only
to be overruled by the War Department. On May 4, Lincoln was laid to rest
in Springfield.

As the war ended, all Americans shared a common sense of having lived
through events that had transformed their world. "Southern newspaper articles

of three or four years ago make me feel very old," New Yorker George Templeton Strong confided in his diary in 1865. "We have lived a century of common life since then." Paradoxically, each side lost something it had gone to war to preserve. Slavery was the cornerstone of the Confederacy, yet the struggle for Southern independence led inexorably to the institution's destruction. The war also caused the death of nearly one-quarter of the South's white men of military age and of tens of thousands of blacks and left countless farms, plantations, businesses, and railroads in ruins. Well into the twentieth century, the South would remain the nation's poorest region. In the North, even as the war vindicated the free labor ideology, it helped transform a society of small producers—from which this ideology had sprung—into an industrial leviathan. As 200,000 Northern soldiers marched in triumph through Washington in the Grand Review of the Union Armies, it was already clear, in the words of abolitionist Wendell Phillips, that Americans were "never again to see the republic in which we were born."

John Wilkes Booth, actor and Confederate sympathizer, assassin of President Lincoln.

The bed on which Lincoln died, from the Peterson home across the street from Ford's Theater, Washington, D.C.

The route of Lincoln's funeral procession in Chicago on May 2, 1865, featured a large Gothic arch draped in black crepe and topped with an eagle figure. A horse-drawn hearse, accompanied by young women dressed in white, carried the coffin to the Chicago Court House, where the president lay in state overnight.

A postwar photograph of Mary Livermore.

MARY RICE LIVERMORE
(1820–1905)

Mary Livermore played an important role in civilian efforts to support the Union cause. Born in Boston, she worked as a teacher before settling in Chicago with her husband, a Universalist minister. When the war broke out she volunteered to work for the U.S. Sanitary Commission, an organization affiliated with the War Department that established hospitals and gathered medical and other supplies for soldiers.

In 1862 and 1863 Livermore toured military hospitals to assess conditions and needs, while also ministering to injured and dying soldiers. Along with her friend and co-worker Mary Hoge, she organized two fairs for the Sanitary Commission in Chicago, which raised nearly $400,000 for soldiers' aid.

Like many other Northern women, Livermore emerged from the war with experience in public affairs and a deep resentment against her legal and political subordination to men. She organized the state's first woman suffrage convention and urged women to seek higher education. The days "of tutelage seem to be ended," she wrote; and women must "think and act for themselves."

A black artisan, urbanite, and soldier, all depicted as newly enfranchised citizens in The First Vote *(1867).*

SEVEN

THE WAR'S AFTERMATH

The Civil War settled two divisive questions—the permanence of the Union and the fate of slavery—only to raise a host of others. Who should control the South? What should be the status of the former slaves? What labor system should replace slavery? On these questions the contentious politics of the Reconstruction era persistently turned.

Central to the national debate over Reconstruction was the effort by Southern blacks to breathe full meaning into their newly acquired freedom. Blacks seized the opportunity created by the end of slavery to consolidate their families and communities, establish a network of churches and other autonomous institutions, stake a claim to equal citizenship, and carve out as much independence as possible in their working lives. Just as during the Civil War the actions of slaves helped force the nation down the road to emancipation, the freedmen's quest for individual and community autonomy did much to establish Reconstruction's political and economic agenda.

Lincoln did not approach the postwar period with a fixed plan of Reconstruction. During the Civil War he had experimented with a number of approaches, but all had remained subordinate to the primary objective of securing military victory. In his last speech, delivered at the White House three days before his assassination, Lincoln for the first time endorsed the idea that some Southern blacks—he specified "the very intelligent" and "those who serve our cause as soldiers"—should be granted the vote and a role in shaping their region's postwar public life. His position reflected a growing consensus within the Republican party that the federal government had a responsibility to protect the basic rights of Southern freedmen, although disagreement remained regarding the vote. Radical Republicans like Thaddeus Stevens and Charles Sumner had long insisted that without black suffrage the old planter class would resume its accustomed power and the former slaves would be unable to defend themselves against injustice. The Union's victory in the Civil War, they believed, created a golden opportunity to purge the nation of "the demon of caste" and to create what Stevens called a "perfect republic" based on the principle of equal rights.

Partly because of the contribution black soldiers had made to the war effort, many moderate Republicans had come to believe that although voting qualifications should remain a matter for the states to determine, the federal government should guarantee the equality before the law of all citizens, regardless of race, and their equal opportunity to compete for economic advancement. Reflecting the growing conviction that blacks had earned a claim upon the conscience of the nation, a number of Northern states took small but significant steps in 1865 toward easing the color line. Several major cities desegregated their streetcars, and Illinois repealed its laws prohibiting blacks from entering the state, serving on juries, and testifying in court.

The man who succeeded Lincoln in the White House proved incapable of providing the reunited nation with enlightened leadership, or of meeting the Republican North's demand for a just and lasting Reconstruction. Andrew Johnson had risen to prominence before the war as a spokesman for the Tennessee yeomanry and a severe critic of the planter class, which he called a "pampered, bloated, corrupted aristocracy." As the only senator from a seceding state to remain at his post in 1861, Johnson had become a symbol of beleaguered Southern Unionism, and his nomination as vice president in 1864 reflected Republicans' determination to extend their organization into the South once the war had ended. To Johnson, Reconstruction offered an opportunity for nonslaveholders to assume control of Southern affairs. The freedmen had no role to play in his vision of a reconstructed South. When a delegation of blacks, including Frederick Douglass and John Jones, visited him at the White House in February 1866 to press their demand for equal rights, Johnson proposed that their people emigrate to some other country. He believed that blacks in the meantime should labor contentedly for their old masters and leave political affairs to whites.

Johnson launched his plan of Reconstruction in May 1865, while Congress was out of session. He appointed provisional governors for the Southern states and conferred a blanket pardon on former Confederates who took an oath affirming their loyalty to the Union and support for emancipation. High Confederate officials and owners of property valued at more than $20,000 were excluded but could apply for individual pardons, which Johnson granted in profusion. Once each Southern state established a new government that acknowledged the illegality of secession and the abolition of slavery, it would be entitled to resume

After its defeat in the Civil War, the South recalled the Confederacy as "The Lost Cause." This 1871 lithograph, with the fading stars and bars of the Confederate flag in the distance, depicts the loss of loved ones and of a way of life.

its place within the Union. Johnson's Reconstruction was for whites only: he not only denied blacks the franchise but ordered that former slaves be evicted from lands they occupied at the end of the war, including plantations from which the owners had fled and the thousands of acres on which freedmen had been settled by the Union Army.

Given a free hand in shaping the transition from slavery to freedom, the new Southern governments adopted a series of laws known as the Black Codes, aimed, as a Louisiana Republican complained, at "getting things back as near to slavery as possible." Blacks were required to possess, each January, written evidence of employment; anyone who failed to sign a labor contract or left a job before the end of the year could be arrested for vagrancy and forced to labor for a white person who would pay the fine. No such laws applied to white citizens. Some states authorized the apprenticing of black youngsters to white employers without the consent of their parents; others forbade blacks from renting land. These laws were enforced by a judicial system in which blacks had no voice, since they could neither testify against whites nor serve on juries, and by all-white militias that often consisted of Confederate veterans still wearing their gray uniforms. In many parts of the South, governmental efforts to relegate blacks to a subordinate position were supplemented by a campaign of violence that attempted to force freedmen to abandon the idea of equality and return to disciplined labor on the plantations.

When Congress assembled in December 1865, Johnson announced that Reconstruction was complete, since governments loyal to the Union existed in all the Southern states. But the policies of the governments Johnson had established seemed to make a mockery of principles crucial to all Republicans: loyalty to the Union, emancipation, and the rights of free labor. The Republican majority refused to seat the newly elected Southern congressmen (many of whom had been high-ranking Confederate officials) and proceeded to demand modifications in the president's program. Johnson, however, proved as stubborn as Lincoln had been flexible; once Johnson announced a policy, he was unwilling to modify it in any way. It was only over the president's veto that one of the

Long after the war ended, Northerners and Southerners commemorated the fallen soldiers. This 1884 photograph with portrait, riderless horse, and an American flag, pays tribute to William Henry Lamb of Ottawa, Illinois.

most significant pieces of legislation of the nineteenth century became law—
the Civil Rights Act of 1866. This defined all persons born in the United States
(except Indians) as national citizens and spelled out rights they were to enjoy
equally without regard to race: making contracts, bringing lawsuits, and enjoying
"full and equal benefit of all laws and proceedings for the security of person
and property." No state law or custom could deprive any citizen of what Illinois
Senator Lyman Trumbull, the law's author, called these "fundamental rights
belonging to every man as a free man."

The first attempt to define in legislative terms the essence of freedom and
the common rights of American citizenship, the Civil Rights Act radically transformed the legal status of blacks throughout the nation. It was quickly followed
by congressional approval of the Fourteenth Amendment, which established the
primacy of national citizenship and prohibited the states from violating any
American's civil rights. Three years later, the Fifteenth Amendment barred the
states from abridging the right to vote because of race. Carrying forward the
nation-building process catalyzed by the Civil War, the Reconstruction Amendments represented a fundamental change in America's constitutional system.
The nation's founders had viewed centralized power as the greatest threat to
individual liberty, a position reflected in the Bill of Rights, which barred Congress but not the states from abridging freedom of speech and other fundamental
rights. During the war Republicans had come to view the federal government
as the "custodian of liberty" rather than a threat to it, and the amendments
empowered the nation to define and protect the rights of all American citizens.

Johnson denounced the Fourteenth Amendment as a violation of the states'
traditional rights, and all the Southern states but Tennessee refused to ratify it.
Their course persuaded Congress that only a complete change in local government could bring "loyal" men to power in the South and guarantee the freedmen's fundamental rights. In 1867, over Johnson's veto, it mandated the
establishment of new Southern governments based on the principle of universal
manhood suffrage. There followed the period of Radical Reconstruction (1867–
1877), in which blacks for the first time in American history voted in large
numbers, served on juries, and held major political offices. Fourteen blacks sat
in the House of Representatives during these years, and Hiram Revels and
Blanche K. Bruce represented Mississippi in the Senate. At the state level, blacks
held positions as lieutenant governor, secretary of state, and superintendent of
education, and some 600 sat in Southern legislatures. Hundreds more served
as justices of the peace, on school boards, and in other local offices.

Blacks and their white allies—newcomers from the North, "carpetbaggers"
to their political foes, and Southern whites willing to accept the new order of
things, castigated as "scalawags"—created Republican organizations that, for a
time, enjoyed political power in every Southern state except Virginia. These
governments dramatically increased the scope of Southern public authority,

Disguised members of the Ku Klux Klan, as depicted in Harper's Weekly *in 1868.*

establishing the region's first state-funded public school systems, enacting sweeping civil rights laws, and seeking to promote Southern economic development. They abolished imprisonment for debt, expanded the legal rights of Southern women, assumed responsibility for assisting the poor, and sought to ensure fair treatment of laborers.

Still, in some ways Reconstruction proved a disappointment to the former slaves. It failed to provide an economic underpinning for their freedom, leaving most blacks as impoverished agricultural laborers compelled by necessity to work on plantations owned by whites. Yet the experiment in interracial democracy was such a departure from American traditions that it provoked violent resistance in the South and, by the 1870s, a national retreat from Reconstruction. In the former Confederate states, the Ku Klux Klan and kindred organizations embarked on a campaign of terror, targeting local Republican leaders for assassination or brutal beatings and assaulting blacks who tried to exercise the right to vote or to establish their economic independence. Violence enabled the Democrats to regain political power in several Southern states. And the continued turmoil in the South, coupled with reports of widespread corruption, led increasing numbers of Northerners to tire of the whole experiment, or to blame Reconstruction's problems on the former slaves' alleged incapacity for government.

In the winter of 1876–77, sixteen years after the secession crisis, the nation again confronted a political impasse when the presidential election failed to produce an undisputed winner. Both Republican Rutherford B. Hayes and Democrat Samuel J. Tilden claimed victory, with the outcome hinging on disputed returns from Louisiana, South Carolina, and Florida, where Republicans still held power. In the end a compromise resolved the crisis. Hayes became president, while Democrats assumed control in the three Southern states. The Bargain of 1877 marked a definitive end to Reconstruction and with it national protection of the former slaves' civil and political rights.

By this time the Civil War had entered the historical memory of both sections. In the North, the Grand Army of the Republic, the organization of war veterans, became a fixture of Republican politics and a presence in every Northern community. Even as the Republican party abandoned its early idealism, the loyalties created by the war helped it retain national dominance into the twentieth century. In the South, the Confederate experience was remembered as the Lost Cause, a noble struggle for local rights and individual liberty (with the defense of slavery conveniently forgotten).

By the turn of the century, as soldiers from North and South fought side by side in the Spanish-American War, it seemed that the nation had put the bitterness of the 1860s behind it. But the road to reunion was paved with black Americans' shattered dreams. With Northern acquiescence the Solid South, now uniformly Democratic, nullified the Fourteenth and Fifteenth amendments and

The right of United States citizens to vote, guaranteed regardless of "race, color, or previous condition of servitude" by ratification of the 15th Amendment in 1870, is commemorated in this lithograph.

imposed a new racial order based on disenfranchisement, segregation, and economic inequality.

Just as the Revolution bequeathed to nineteenth-century Americans the problem of slavery, the Civil War era left to future generations the implementation of some of the basic principles for which the war had been fought.

FURTHER READING

The Civil War era has been the subject of a voluminous literature, including some of the finest works of American history ever written. This list offers only a brief sampling of the most significant recent works.

Allan Nevins's eight-volume *Ordeal of the Union* (New York, 1947–71) remains the best overall account of the period. For one-volume studies, see David H. Donald, *Liberty and Union* (New York, 1978), and Richard Sewell, *A House Divided* (Baltimore, 1988).

Kenneth Stampp, *The Peculiar Institution* (New York, 1956), remains the best overall introduction to the institution of slavery. Eugene Genovese explores the economics of slavery in *The Political Economy of Slavery* (New York, 1965) and the lives of the slaves in *Roll, Jordan, Roll* (New York, 1974). Herbert Gutman, *The Black Family in Slavery and Freedom* (New York, 1976), is among the finest recent studies of slave culture, while Jacqueline Jones, *Labor of Love, Labor of Sorrow* (New York, 1985), discusses the experience of black women during and after slavery. For resistance to slavery, Herbert Aptheker, *American Negro Slave Revolts* (New York, 1943), remains the starting point. Ira Berlin, *Slaves Without Masters* (New York, 1974), is the best survey of the status of free blacks in the antebellum South. There are few recent studies of nonslaveholding whites, but see Steven Hahn, *The Roots of Southern Populism* (New York, 1983). An excellent recent account of slavery in one locality is J. William Harris, *Plain Folk and Gentry in a Slave Society* (Middletown, Conn., 1986).

Thomas Cochran, *Frontiers of Change* (New York, 1981), offers a brief survey of America's economic development in these years. Still valuable is the older study, *The Transportation Revolution* (New York, 1951), by George Rogers Taylor. Richard Bartlett, *The New Country* (New York, 1979), is an excellent survey of westward expansion, including its impact upon American Indians. See also Ray Billington, *The Far Western Frontier* (New York, 1956). Sean Wilentz, *Chants Democratic* (New York, 1984), is the best study of changes in the work process and the early labor movement, while Catherine Clinton, *The Other Civil War* (New York, 1984), surveys the changing role of women in nineteenth-century America. For the impact of social change on Jacksonian politics, see Marvin Meyers, *The Jacksonian Persuasion* (Stanford, 1957), and Edward Pessen, *Jacksonian America* (New York, 1977). John W. Ward, *Andrew Jackson: Symbol for an Age* (New York, 1955), is a good introduction to the cultural meanings of Jacksonian politics.

Ronald Walters, *American Reformers* (New York, 1978), offers a brief introduction to antebellum reform movements. The best study of the Nullification Crisis is William Freehling, *Prelude to Civil War* (New York, 1965). On abolitionism, see James Stewart, *Holy Warriors* (New York, 1976), and Aileen Kraditor, *Means and Ends in American Abolitionism* (New York, 1969). Vincent Harding, *There Is a River* (New York, 1981), discusses the black abolitionists. The early women's rights movement is examined in Ellen DuBois, *Feminism and Suffrage* (Ithaca, 1978), while Leon Litwack, *North of Slavery* (Chicago, 1961), explores Northern racism before the Civil War. For anti-abolitionist violence, see Leonard Richards, *Gentlemen of Property and Standing* (New York, 1967). Robert Johannsen, *To the Halls of Montezuma* (New York, 1985), discusses the impact of the Mexican War on the American imagination. For the rise of the free soil issue, the Compromise of 1850, and Kansas-Nebraska, see David Potter, *The Impending Crisis* (New York, 1976). Eric Foner, *Free Soil, Free Labor, Free Men* (New York, 1970), studies the ideas of the early Republican party.

Don Fehrenbacher, *The Dred Scott Case* (New York, 1978), provides a full examination of that pivotal decision. For Lincoln in the 1850s, see Fehrenbacher's *Prelude to Greatness* (Stanford, 1962). The most recent biography of Lincoln is Stephen Oates's *With Malice Toward None* (New York, 1977). Michael Holt, *The Political Crisis of the 1850s* (New York, 1978), gives a sense of the Democrats' ideas. Robert Johannsen, *Stephen A. Douglas* (New York, 1973), is the best biography of the "Little Giant," while Stephen Oates, *To Purge This Land with Blood* (New York, 1970), offers an excellent portrait of John Brown. For the rise of secession sentiment, see John McCardell, *The Idea of a Southern Nation* (New York, 1979), and William Barney, *The Road to Secession* (New York, 1975). Kenneth Stampp, *And the War Came* (New York, 1950), discusses the secession crisis.

James McPherson, *Battle Cry of Freedom* (New York, 1988), is the best one-volume survey of the Civil War. More detailed is Shelby Foote's excellent three-volume series, *The Civil War* (New York, 1958–74). Two studies that offer explanations of the war's outcome are Herman Hattaway and Archer Jones, *How the North Won* (Urbana, 1983), and Richard E. Beringer, Herman Hattaway, Archer Jones, and William Still, Jr., *Why the South Lost the Civil War* (Athens, Ga., 1986). For the experience of ordinary soldiers, see Gerald F. Linderman, *Embattled Courage* (New York, 1987), and Reid Mitchell, *Civil War Soldiers* (New York, 1988). Edward Hagerman, *The American Civil War and the Origins of Modern Warfare* (Bloomington, In., 1988), discusses the war as a modern conflict. T. Harry Williams, *Lincoln and His Generals* (New York, 1952), examines Lincoln's military leadership. Bruce Catton's three-volume work, *The Centennial History of the Civil War* (New York, 1961–65), traces the war's military progress in vivid prose. William McFeely, *Grant* (New York, 1981), is the best biography of the North's greatest general, while Thomas Connelly, *The Marble Man* (New York, 1977), is an interesting evaluation of the changing image of Lee. William Frassanito, *Antietam* (New York, 1978), discusses the battle and the development of Civil War photography.

The coming of emancipation and the experience of black soldiers are treated in Ira Berlin, et al., eds., *Freedom: A Documentary History of Emancipation* (New York, 1982–   ). LaWanda Cox, *Lincoln and Black Freedom* (Columbia, S.C., 1981), traces the evolution of Lincoln's views, while Hans L. Trefousse, *The Radical Republicans* (New York, 1969), examines this pivotal group. For the wartime North, see Philip Paludan, *A People's Contest* (New York, 1989), and George Fredrickson, *The Inner Civil War* (New York, 1965). For the Southern home front, see Emory Thomas, *The Confederate Nation* (New York, 1979). Iver Bernstein, *The New York City Draft Riots* (New York, 1989), chronicles turmoil in the North, while Paul Escott, *After Secession* (New York, 1978), traces the rise of disaffection in the wartime South. The end of the war is treated in Joseph T. Glatthaar, *The March to the Sea and Beyond* (New York, 1985), and A. A. Hoehling and Mary Hoehling, *The Day Richmond Died* (San Diego, 1981).

Eric Foner, *Reconstruction: America's Unfinished Revolution* (New York, 1988), is the most up-to-date study of the postwar years; an abridged edition is available as *A Short History of Reconstruction* (New York, 1990). For the black experience in the transition from slavery to freedom, see Leon Litwack, *Been in the Storm so Long* (New York, 1979). Eric McKitrick, *Andrew Johnson and Reconstruction* (Chicago, 1961), and W. R. Brock, *An American Crisis* (New York, 1963), examine the impasse between Johnson and Congress, while Harold Hyman and William Wiecek, *Equal Justice Under Law* (New York, 1982), is the best study of the constitutional and legal changes of the Reconstruction years. For the Ku Klux Klan, see Allen W. Trelease, *White Terror* (New York, 1971). The abandonment of Reconstruction is traced in William Gillette, *Retreat from Reconstruction* (Baton Rouge, 1979), while C. Vann Woodward, *Origins of the New South* (Baton Rouge, 1951), makes clear some of its consequences. Gaines Foster, *Ghosts of the Confederacy* (New York, 1986), examines the rise of the idea of the Lost Cause.

CHECKLIST OF
THE EXHIBITION

The following is a checklist of artifacts in the permanent exhibition *A House Divided: America in the Age of Lincoln*, on view at the Chicago Historical Society for a ten-year period beginning in January 1990. The checklist organization reflects the seven major sections of the exhibition: The "Peculiar Institution"; Lincoln's America; The Slavery Controversy; The Impending Crisis; The Civil War: The First Modern War; War, Politics, and Society; and The Aftermath. Each checklist entry includes all known information about the object, including artist, maker, or author; artist's birth and death dates; date and place of manufacture or publication; medium; dimensions; provenance; and catalogue number. All dimensions are given in inches and centimeters; height precedes width. Unless otherwise noted, dimensions for paintings include the period frame. ICHi numbers are copy negative numbers for materials in the Society's Prints and Photographs Collection. All other numbers are accession numbers for materials from the Society's collections.

ONE THE "PECULIAR INSTITUTION"

An American Slave Market
Painting
Taylor
1852
Oil on canvas
33⅛ × 44¼ in.; 84.1 × 104.8 cm.
Gift of Ellen N. LaMotte
1954.15

After the Sale: Slaves Going South from Richmond
Painting
Eyre Crowe (1824–1910)
1853
Oil on canvas
27⅜ × 36⅛ in.; 69.5 × 91.8 cm.
1957.27

"Will. Boyd, Jr. General Agents & Dealer in
Negroes"
Trade card
c. 1845
Ink on paper
3⅛ × 2⅝ in.; 7.9 × 6.7 cm.

10 Likely and Valuable Slaves at Auction
Broadside
1823
Ink on paper
11⅜ × 8⅞ in.; 28.9 × 22.5 cm.
ICHi-22000

Credit Sale of a Choice Gang of 41 Slaves!
Broadside
1856
Ink on paper
18⅝ × 11⅞ in.; 47.3 × 30.2 cm.
Gift of Laura Hoffman
ICHi-22001

Public Sale of Negroes
Broadside
1833
Ink on paper
12 × 8¼ in.; 30.5 × 21 cm.
Gift of Peter W. Rooney
ICHi-22002

Sale of Slaves and Stock
Broadside
1852
Ink on paper
12⅝ × 8⅛ in.; 32.1 × 20.6 cm.
Gift of Peter W. Rooney
ICHi-22003

Leg Shackles
c. 1850
Iron
a) 28 × 4 × 1 in.; 71.1 × 10.2 × 2.5 cm.
b) 24 × 2 × 4 in.; 61 × 5.1 × 10.2 cm.
a) X.1354
b) XA-2019

Arm Shackles
c. 1850
Iron
12 × 3 × 1⅝ in.; 30.5 × 7.6 × 4.1 cm.
Charles F. Gunther Collection
1920.1716

Account Book
Hector Davis & Company, Richmond, Virginia
1857–1860
Ink on paper, leather binding
16 × 11½ × 22½ in.; 40.6 × 29.2 × 57.2 cm.
Charles F. Gunther Collection

Plantation Hoe
W. Alyndon, England
c. 1850
Iron
8⅝ × 5 × 1⅝ in.; 21.9 × 12.7 × 4.1 cm.
Gift of Dr. John M. Pillsbury
1923.84

Slave Shoes
c. 1860
Leather, wood, iron
3 × 4 × 12 in.; 7.6 × 10.2 × 30.5 cm.
Charles F. Gunther Collection

Scenes on a Cotton Plantation
Wood engraving from sketches by Alfred R.
Waud
Harper's Weekly
February 2, 1867
Ink on paper
15⅞ × 20½ in.; 40.3 × 52.1 cm.

Cotton Pressing in Louisiana
Wood engraving from sketches by A. Hill
Ballou's Magazine
April 12, 1856
Ink on paper
5⅛ × 9¼ in.; 13 × 25.5 cm.

Bond for $150 to Robert E. Lee for the Hire "of
his Negro Boy, Harrison"
Manuscript
January 2, 1860
Ink on paper
10 × 7⅞ in.; 25.4 × 20 cm.
Charles F. Gunther Collection

Slave Tag, "Porter"
1857
Copper
1⅝ × 1⅝ in.; 4.1 × 4.1 cm.
Charles F. Gunther Collection
1920.1274

Slave Tag, "Servant"
1837
Copper
1⅞ × 1⅞ in.; 4.8 × 4.8 cm.
Charles F. Gunther Collection
1920.986

Slave Tag, "Porter"
1829
Copper
2 × 2⅛ in.; 5.1 × 5.4 cm.
Charles F. Gunther Collection
1920.7

Slave Tag, "Servant"
1860
Copper
1½ × 1½ in.; 3.8 × 3.8 cm.
Charles F. Gunther Collection
1920.1273

Slave Tag, "Servant"
1847
Copper
1¾ × 1¾ in.; 4.4 × 4.4 cm.
Charles F. Gunther Collection
1920.1732

Slave Tag, "Porter"
1831
Copper
2⅛ × 2⅛ in.; 5.4 × 5.4 cm.
Charles F. Gunther Collection
1920.1733

Slave Tag, "Porter"
1817
Copper
2⅛ × 2⅛ in.; 5.4 × 5.4 cm.
Charles F. Gunther Collection
1920.6

Slave Tag, "Fruiterer"
1863
Copper
1½ × 1⅛ in.; 3.8 × 2.9 cm.
Charles F. Gunther Collection
1920.991

"Insurrection of the Blacks"
Newspaper article
Niles Weekly Register
September 3, 1831
Ink on paper
9¾ × 6⅝ in.; 24.8 × 16.8 cm.
Gift of The Pond Bequest

*Joseph Cinquez Addressing His Compatriots on
Board the Spanish Schooner,* Armstad, *26th
Aug. 1839*
Lithograph
John Childs
1839
Ink on paper
10½ × 16⅝ in.; 26.7 × 42.2 cm.
Charles F. Gunther Collection
ICHi-22004

100 Dolls. Reward
Broadside
c. 1855
Ink on paper
12 × 9⅜ in.; 30.5 × 23.8 cm.
ICHi-22005

$300 Reward
Broadside
1855
Ink on paper
9⅞ × 7¾ in.; 25.1 × 19.7 cm.
ICHi-22006

200 Dollars Reward!
Broadside
1850
Ink on paper
12 × 9½ in.; 30.5 × 24.1 cm.
ICHi-22007

100 Dollars Reward
Broadside
1857
Ink on paper
12 × 9¾ in.; 30.5 × 24.8 cm.
ICHi-22008

Narrative of the Life of Frederick Douglass
Book
Frederick Douglass
Publisher: Anti-Slavery Office, Boston
1845
Ink on paper
7⅛ × 4⅞ in.; 18.1 × 12.4 cm. (closed)
7⅛ × 9⅛ in.; 18.1 × 23.2 cm. (open)

Portrait of Frederick Douglass
Steel engraving from *Narrative of the Life of Frederick Douglass*
Publisher: Anti-Slavery Office, Boston
1845
Ink on paper
6¾ × 4 in.; 17.1 × 10.2 cm.

"The Fugitive's Song"
Sheet music
Jesse Hutchinson, Jr.
Publisher: Henry Prentiss, Boston
1845
Ink on paper
14 × 10¾ in.; 35.6 × 27.3 cm.

Douglass' Monthly
Newspaper
Editor: Frederick Douglass, Rochester New York
December 1860
Ink on paper
12⅞ × 8½ in.; 32.7 × 21.6 cm.

*The Negro in His Own Country
The Negro in America*
Wood engravings from *Bible Defence of Slavery; or the Origin, History, and Fortunes of the Negro Race*
Josiah Priest
Publisher: Rev. W. S. Brown, Glasgow, Kentucky
1853
Ink on paper
9⅜ × 6⅜ in.; 23.8 × 16.2 cm.

Bible Defence of Slavery; or the Origin, History, and Fortunes of the Negro Race
Book
Josiah Priest
Publisher: Rev. W. S. Brown, Glasgow, Kentucky
1853
Ink on paper
9½ × 6⅛ × 1⅜ in.; 24.1 × 15.6 × 3.5 cm.

Sociology for the South, or the Failure of Free Society
Pamphlet
George Fitzhugh
Publisher: A. Morris, Richmond, Virginia
1854
Ink on paper
7⅝ × 9⅛ in.; 19.4 × 23.2 cm. (open)

Cotton Crop of the United States
Broadside
Office of the Shipping and Commercial List, New York
1850
Ink on paper
12¼ × 9 in.; 31.1 × 22.9 cm.
ICHi-22009

"Old King Cotton"
Sheet music
George P. Morris and Wm. H. Morris
Publisher: Wm. Hall & Son, New York
1860
Ink on paper
14⅛ × 10⅞ in.; 35.9 × 27.6 cm.

View of the Famous Levee of New Orleans
Wood engraving from a photograph by E. H. Nelson, Jr.
Frank Leslie's Illustrated Newspaper
April 14, 1860
Ink on paper
16⅝ × 22¾ in.; 42.2 × 57.8 cm.

Cotton Is King and Pro-Slavery Arguments
Pamphlet
E. N. Elliott
Publisher: Pritchard, Abbott & Loomis, Augusta, Georgia
1860
Ink on paper
10 × 7 × 3 in.; 25.7 × 17.8 × 7.6 cm.

TWO *LINCOLN'S AMERICA*

"Outline Map of Indian Localities in 1833"
Map from *Illustrations of the Manners, Customs, and Condition of the North American Indian*, by George Catlin
Publisher: Chatto & Windus, London
1876
Ink on paper
9½ × 14⅞ in.; 24.1 × 37.8 cm.

Portrait of Black Hawk
Painting after a portrait by Charles Bird King, 1837
Homer Henderson
c. 1870
Oil on canvas
36⅛ × 30⅛ in.; 91.8 × 76.5 cm.
Gift of William H. Bush
1920.557

.69 Caliber Flintlock Musket
Springfield Armory
1829
Walnut, steel, flint
57⅛ × 6 × 3 in.; 145.1 × 15.2 × 7.6 cm.
Charles F. Gunther Collection
1920.493

Wampum (allegedly belonged to Black Hawk)
c. 1832
Shell, twine, tobacco, cloth
Length: 21⅛ in.; 53.7 cm.
X.1212

Life of Black Hawk
Book
Black Hawk
Publisher: Richard James Kennett, London
1836
Ink on paper
7 × 8¼ in.; 17.8 × 21 cm. (open)

Death Mask of Black Hawk
1838
Painted plaster
9⅞ × 5⅞ × 3¾ in.; 25.1 × 14.9 × 9.5 cm.
Gift of Paul H. Gundersen
1963.341

O-Che-Na-Shink-Kaa
Color lithograph after a painting by James Otto Lewis (1799–1858)
Lithographers: Lehman & Duval, Philadelphia
1835
Ink on paper
18 × 11 in.; 45.7 × 27.9 cm.
ICHi-22213

A Sioux Chief
Color lithograph after a painting by
 James Otto Lewis (1799–1858)
Lithographers: Lehman & Duval, Philadelphia
1835
Ink on paper
18 × 11 in.; 45.7 × 27.9 cm.
ICHi-22214

Chat-O-Nis-Sec
Color lithograph after a painting by
 James Otto Lewis (1799–1858)
Lithographers: Lehman & Duval, Philadelphia
1835
Ink on paper
18 × 11 in.; 45.7 × 27.9 cm.
ICHi-22215

Prof. Samuel F. B. Morse
Steel engraving
John Starton
c. 1850
Ink on paper
12 × 9⅛ in.; 30.5 × 23.2 cm.

Canal Scene/Moonlight
Color lithograph
Currier & Ives, New York
1838–1856
Ink on paper
10⅞ × 14 in.; 27.6 × 35.6 cm.
Gift of Mrs. Stuyvesant Peabody
ICHi-22010

For Chicago
Broadside
E. A. Maynard & Co. Printers, Buffalo
1848
Ink on paper
9¾ × 7⅞ in.; 24.8 × 20 cm.
ICHi-22128

Eight Daily Lines to Pittsburg and Wheeling
Broadside
Young Printer, Philadelphia
1846
Ink on paper
16⅞ × 7⅜ in.; 42.9 × 18.7 cm.
ICHi-22011

Illinois Central Railroad
Broadside
1853
Ink on paper
19 × 12 in.; 48.3 × 30.5 cm.
Gift of Mr. and Mrs. Richard C. Andersen
ICHi-22012

Grand Trunk Rail Road
Broadside
Henry B. Ashmead, Printers, Philadelphia
1857
Ink on paper
18⅜ × 15⅝ in.; 46.7 × 39.7 cm.
ICHi-22013

View of St. Louis
Color lithograph
Julius Hutawa
c. 1846
Ink on paper
20¼ × 23½ in.; 51.4 × 59.7 cm.
Gift of Charles B. Pike
1940.18
ICHi-22019

Cincinnati in 1840
Color lithograph
Klauprech & Menzel
1840
7¾ × 15 in.; 19.7 × 38.1 cm.
Gift of Charles B. Pike
1941.160
ICHi-22015

View of Chicago
Color lithograph
Ed. Mendel, Chicago
Publisher: Rufus Blanchard, Chicago
c. 1854
Ink on paper
11½ × 19⅝ in.; 29.2 × 49.8 cm.
1950.159
ICHi-22152

View of New York. From Brooklyn Heights
Color lithograph
Nathaniel Currier
1849
Ink on paper
13⅞ × 17⅞ in.; 35.2 × 45.4 cm.
Gift of Charles B. Pike
1929.90
ICHi-22129

Model of the 1831 McCormick Reaper
McCormick Works, Chicago
1931
Wood, metal, machine castings, canvas
16 × 13½ × 35 in.; 40.6 × 34.3 × 88.9 cm.
Gift of Cyrus H. McCormick, Harold F.
 McCormick, and Mrs. Emmons Blaine
1931.31

*McCormicks' Patent Reaping and Mowing
 Machine!*
Broadside
Journal Office Printers, Chicago
1853
Ink on paper
17¼ × 11¾ in.; 43.8 × 29.8 cm.
ICHi-22016

*Wemple's Separators . . . Chicago Threshing
 Machine Manufactory*
Broadside
1851
Ink on paper
21½ × 13⅝ in.; 54.6 × 34.6 cm.
Gift of Eugene J. Trudeau
ICHi-22127

*View in the Machine Shop of Silas C. Herring &
 Co.*
Wood engraving
Frank Leslie's Illustrated Newspaper
August 15, 1857
Ink on paper
6¾ × 10¾ in.; 17.1 × 27.3 cm.

The Shoemaker's Strike at Lynn, Mass.
Wood engraving
Frank Leslie's Illustrated Newspaper
March 17, 1860
Ink on paper
16½ × 11¼ in.; 41.9 × 28.6 cm.

.52 Caliber Rifle and Bayonet
J. H. Hall, Harper's Ferry Arsenal, Virginia
U.S. Model 1819, made in 1832
Walnut, steel
Overall length: 18½ in.; 47 cm.
Gift of Elmer P. Renstrom, Jr.
1955.110ab

Dishes
Boston & Sandwich Glass Company, Sandwich,
 Massachusetts
1830–1840
Pressed glass
a) Diameter: 7¼ in.; 18.4 cm.
b) Diameter: 6⅞ in.; 17.5 cm.
a) 1972.199
b) 1972.200

Cup Plates (9)
Boston & Sandwich Glass Company, Sandwich,
 Massachusetts
1825–1850
Pressed glass
Diameters: 3–3¼ in.;
Gift of Suzanne Swift and Howard G. Rose

Oval Dishes
Boston & Sandwich Glass Company, Sandwich,
 Massachusetts
c. 1825
Pressed glass
6¼ × 3⅞ × 1½ in.; 15.9 × 9.8 × 3.8 cm.
Gift of Suzanne Swift
1969.1561

Deming Jarvis Presentation Goblet
Boston & Sandwich Glass Company, Sandwich,
 Massachusetts
c. 1858
Pressed glass
6¼ × 3¼ in.; 15.9 × 8.3 cm.
Gift of Mrs. Russell A. Alger
1935.80

Salt Dish
Boston & Sandwich Glass Company, Sandwich,
    Massachusetts
c. 1830
Pressed glass
1¾ × 3 in.; 4.4 × 7.6 cm.
Gift of Mrs. Frank L. Sulzberger
1973.19

Sewing Machine
Wheeler and Wilson, Bridgeport, Connecticut
c. 1867
Walnut, iron, steel
42 × 26 × 25 in.; 106.7 × 66 × 63.5 cm.
Gift of David B. Erickson
1957.754

Wheeler and Wilson Sewing Machines
Catalog
1859
Ink on paper
8⅝ × 5½; 21.9 × 14 cm.

Sofa (allegedly from the Lincoln home,
    Springfield, Illinois)
c. 1855
Mahogany, horsehair upholstery
32½ × 27½ × 80½ in.; 82.6 × 69.9 × 204.5
    cm.
Charles F. Gunther Collection
1920.246

Side Chairs (allegedly from the Lincoln home,
    Springfield, Illinois)
c. 1855
Rosewood, horsehair upholstery
34½ × 18½ × 17 in.; 87.6 × 47 × 43.1 cm.
Charles F. Gunther Collection
1920.242 a–d

Rocking Chair (allegedly from the Lincoln
    home, Springfield, Illinois)
c. 1850
Mahogany, horsehair upholstery
38½ × 23 × 19¾ in.; 97.8 × 58.4 × 50.2
    cm.
Charles F. Gunther Collection
1920.243

Chicago Machinery Depot/Woodworth's Patent
    Planing Machine
Wood engraving advertisement from *The Chicago*
    City Directory and Business Advertiser,
    compiled by E. H. Hall
Publisher: Robert Fergus, Book & Job Printer,
    Chicago
1855–1856
8⅝ × 5¼ in.; 21.9 × 13.3 cm.

"Harrison and Tyler Grand Military Waltz"
Sheet music
Osborn Music Saloon, Philadelphia
c. 1840
Ink on paper
14¼ × 11 in.; 36.2 × 27.9 cm.

William Henry Harrison Log Cabin Novelty
1840
Tortoise shell, wood, ribbon ties
5¼ × 6 × 3⅝ in.; 13.3 × 15.2 × 9.2 cm.
X.587

William Henry Harrison Child's Tea Set
John Ridgeway (1786–1860)
Caulden Place Works, near Hanley, England
1840
China
a) Teapot: 4½ × 6¼ × 3¾ in.; 11.4 × 15.9
    × 9.5 cm.
b) Sugar bowl: 3⅞ × 3⅞ × 3¼ in.; 9.8 ×
    9.8 × 8.3 cm.
c) Creamer: 3 × 3⅛ × 2⅜ in.; 7.6 × 7.9 ×
    6 cm.
d) Cup: 1⅞ × 2⅜ in. diameter; 4.8 × 6 cm.
e) Saucer: 3⅞ in. diameter; 9.8 cm.
Gift of Mrs. Jack Klukkert
1972.128a–g

William Henry Harrison Campaign Banner
1840
Cotton
27¾ × 30½ in.; 70.5 × 77.5 cm.
Gift of Mrs. Ruby Holliday
1959.54

Tippecanoe Club!
Broadside
1840
Ink on paper
13¼ × 9⅛ in.; 33.7 × 23.2 cm.
ICHi-22017

Election Ticket, Whig Party—Abraham Lincoln
1846
Ink on paper
6¾ × 3½ in.; 17.1 × 8.9 cm.
ICHi-22018

Portrait of Abraham Lincoln
Copy print from the original daguerreotype
Attributed to: N. H. Shephard, Springfield,
    Illinois
1846
Library of Congress

"Order to the Clerk of the Sangamon Circuit
    Court"
Manuscript
John T. Stuart and Abraham Lincoln
July 16, 1839
Ink on paper
6 × 7⅝ in.; 15.2 × 19.4 cm.
Gift of Mrs. William F. Peterson

The Present Law Office of Abraham Lincoln The
    President Elect
Wood engraving
Frank Leslie's Illustrated Newspaper
December 22, 1860
Ink on paper
5 × 9¼ in.; 12.7 × 23.5 cm.

The Theory and Practice of Surveying (allegedly
    used by Abraham Lincoln)
Book
Robert Gibson
Publisher: Evert Duyckinck, New York
1814
Ink on paper, leather binding
8¾ × 10¼ in.; 22.2 × 26 cm.

Skate Presented by R. C. Reals to Abraham
    Lincoln in Jest of His Large Feet
c. 1850
Wood
22 × 10¼ × 6¾ in.; 55.9 × 26 × 17.1 cm.
Gift of Cornelius P. Van Schaak
1924.39

THREE *THE SLAVERY CONTROVERSY*

Camp Meeting
Color lithograph
Kelloggs & Comstock, Hartford, Connecticut
c. 1846
Ink on paper
10¼ × 14⅛ in.; 26 × 35.6 cm.
ICHi-22019

Declaration of the Anti-Slavery Convention
Broadside
J. R. Sleeper, Philadelphia
1833
Ink on silk
22¼ × 18⅜ in.; 56.5 × 46.7 cm.

Anti-Slavery!
Broadside
c. 1855
Ink on paper
12½ × 17 in.; 31.8 × 43.2 cm.
ICHi-22020

" 'Get Off The Track!' A Song for Emancipation"
Sheet Music
Composer and publisher: Jesse Hutchinson, Jr.
1844
Ink on paper
12¼ × 10 in.; 31.1 × 25.4 cm.

Letters to Catherine E. Beecher, in Reply to an Essay on Slavery and Abolitionism, Addressed to A. E. Grimke
Book
Angelina E. Grimke
1838
Ink on paper
7¼ × 4⅝ in.; 18.4 × 11.7 cm. (closed)
7¼ × 9 in.; 18.4 × 22.9 cm. (open)

Lucretia Mott
Daguerreotype
c. 1850
Glass, leather case
4¾ × 3¾ in.; 12.1 × 9.5 cm.
Charles F. Gunther Collection
ICHi-22021

Narrative of Sojourner Truth, A Northern Slave
Pamphlet
Sojourner Truth (Olive Gilbert)
1860
Ink on paper
7½ × 4¾ in.; 19.1 × 12.1 cm.
Gift of Mrs. E. E. Atwater

Sojourner Truth
Cabinet card
Randall, Detroit, Michigan
1864
Albumen print
6½ × 4¼ in.; 16.5 × 10.8 cm.
Gift of Mrs. W. H. Hall
ICHi-22022

The Life of Josiah Henson
Pamphlet
Josiah Henson
Publisher: Arthur D. Phelps, Boston
1849
Ink on paper
6⅝ × 4¼ in.; 16.8 × 10.8 cm.

The American Churches, the Bulwarks of American Slavery
Pamphlet
James G. Birney
Publisher: Charles Whipple, Newburyport, Massachusetts
1842
Ink on paper
6⅝ × 4¼ in.; 16.8 × 10.8 cm.

Dr. Channing's Last Address
Pamphlet
William Ellery Channing
Publisher: Oliver Johnson, Boston
1842
Ink on paper
6⅝ × 4¼ in.; 16.8 × 10.8 cm.

American Slavery as It Is: Testimony of a Thousand Witnesses
Book
Publisher: American Anti-Slavery Society, New York
1839
Ink on paper
9 × 5¾ in.; 22.9 × 14.6 cm.

The "Infidelity" of Abolitionism
Pamphlet
William Lloyd Garrison
Publisher: American Anti-Slavery Society, New York
1860
Ink on Paper
7¼ × 4⅝ in.; 18.4 × 11.7 cm.

Why Work For The Slave?
Pamphlet
Publisher: American Anti-Slavery Society, New York
1838
Ink on paper
7¼ × 5 in.; 18.4 × 12.7 cm.

The Fugitive Slave Bill: Its History and Unconstitutionality
Pamphlet
Publisher: American and Foreign Anti-Slavery Society, New York
1850
Ink on paper
7⅝ × 4⅝ in.; 19.4 × 11.7 cm.

The Nature, Character, and History of the Anti-Slavery Movement
Pamphlet
Frederick Douglass
Publisher: G. Gallie, Glasgow, Scotland
1855
Ink on paper
8¼ × 10½ in.; 21 × 26.7 cm. (open)

Douglass' Monthly
Newspaper
Editor: Frederick Douglass
October 1860
Ink on paper
12⅞ × 8½ in.; 32.7 × 21.6 cm.

"Minute Book of the Illinois Anti-Slavery Society"
Manuscript
1837–1844
Ink on paper, leather binding
11⅝ × 8⅝ in.; 29.5 × 21.9 cm. (closed)
11⅝ × 16½ in.; 29.5 × 41.9 cm. (open)
Gift of Mrs. A. E. Shader

Printing Press (allegedly used by Elijah P. Lovejoy)
John Wells
c. 1830
Cast iron
71¾ × 39 × 63½ in.; 180.7 × 99 × 161.3 cm.
Charles F. Gunther Collection
1920.894

The Alton Observer
Newspaper
Editor and publisher: Elijah P. Lovejoy
December 8, 1836
Ink on paper
23½ × 18 in.; 59.7 × 45.7 cm.

Attack on the Printing Office of the Alton Observer, *1837*
Lithograph from *The Martyrdom of Lovejoy* by Henry Tanner
Fergus Printing Company, Chicago
1881
Ink on paper
5⅛ × 8⅞ in.; 13 × 22.5 cm.
Gift of Joseph T. Ryerson

Elijah P. Lovejoy Commemorative Plate
c. 1837
Staffordshire china
Diameter: 9⅛ in.; 23.2 cm.
Gift of Charles B. Pike
1933.97

Silhouette of Elijah P. Lovejoy
From *The Martyrdom of Lovejoy* by Henry Tanner
Fergus Printing Company, Chicago
1881
Ink on paper
8½ × 5¼ in.; 21.6 × 13.3 cm.
Gift of Joseph T. Ryerson

Certificates of Freedom for John Jones and Mary Jane Jones
Manuscript
Clerk of the Circuit Court of Madison County, Illinois
November 28, 1844
Ink on paper
a) 9⅞ × 8 in.; 25.1 × 20.3 cm.
b) 9¾ × 7¾ in.; 24.8 × 19.7 cm.
John Jones Collection

John Jones
Painting
Aaron E. Darling
c. 1865
Oil on canvas
46 × 36 in.; 116.8 × 91.4 cm.
Gift of Mrs. L. Jones Lee
1904.18

Mary Richardson Jones
Painting
Aaron E. Darling
c. 1865
Oil on canvas
33½ × 27½ in.; 85.1 × 69.9 cm.
Gift of Mrs. Theodora Lee Purnell
1955.197

The Black Laws of Illinois, Why They Should Be Repealed
Pamphlet
John H. Jones
1864
Ink on paper
8½ × 5⅝ in.; 21.6 × 14.3 cm.
Gift of Mrs. L. Jones Lee

Uncle Tom's Cabin; or, Life Among the Lowly
Book—2 volumes
Harriet Beecher Stowe
Publisher: John P. Jewett & Company, Boston
1852
7⅞ × 5⅜ in.; 20 × 13.7 cm. (closed)
7⅞ × 10 in.; 20 × 25.4 cm. (open)

Harriet Beecher Stowe
Color steel engraving
From an original drawing by Dennis after daguerreotypes published by
T. H. Ellis
1853
Ink on paper
13 × 7¾ in.; 33 × 19.7 cm.

Letter of Praise from Henry Wadsworth Longfellow to Harriet Beecher Stowe for *Uncle Tom's Cabin*
Henry Wadsworth Longfellow
October 5, 1852
Ink on paper
7¼ × 4½ in.; 18.4 × 11.4 cm.

Perilous Escape of Eliza and Child
Color lithograph
T. W. Strong, New York
c. 1855
Ink on paper
16⅛ × 12⅛ in.; 41 × 30.8 cm.
ICHi-22023

First Meeting of Uncle Tom and Eva
Color lithograph
T. W. Strong, New York
c. 1855
Ink on paper
16⅛ × 12⅛ in.; 41 × 30.8 cm.
ICHi-22024

"An Act To Prevent the Immigration of Free Negroes Into This State"
In *General Laws of the State of Illinois, Passed by the Eighteenth General Assembly, Convened January 3, 1853*
Publisher: Lanphier & Walker, Springfield, Illinois
February 12, 1853
Ink on paper
8¾ × 6⅛ in.; 22.2 × 15.6 cm. (closed)
8¾ × 13⅝ in.; 22.2 × 34.6 cm. (open)

"Zip Coon, A Favorite Comic Song"
Sheet music
Publisher: J. L. Hewitt & Co., New York
1834
Ink on paper
13½ × 9⅞ in.; 34.3 × 25.1 cm.

"Jim Crow"
Sheet music
Publisher: Firth & Hall, New York
1829
Ink on paper
13⅛ × 10⅛ in.; 33.3 × 25.7 cm.

"Christy's Melodies"
Sheet music cover
Edwin P. Christy
Publisher: Jague & Brothers, New York
1847
Ink on paper
12⅞ × 9½ in.; 32.7 × 24.1 cm.
ICHi-22025

"Philadelphia Fashions"
Sheet music cover
Publisher: H. R. Robinson, New York
1837
Ink on paper
14⅞ × 11⅛ in.; 37.8 × 28.3 cm.
ICHi-22026

Map of the United States, 1848
From *The Universal Historical Atlas* by J. W. Sheahan
1873
Ink on paper
17¾ × 24 in.; 45.1 × 61.0 cm.

Surveyor's Compass
E. & G. W. Blunt, New York
c. 1845
Compass: brass, glass
Box: wood, brass
Compass: 2½ × 15¼ × 6⅛ in.; 6.4 × 38.7 × 15.6 cm.
Box: 3¼ × 15⅞ × 7⅜ in.; 8.3 × 40.3 × 18.7 cm.
Gift of Mrs. Walter Chadband
1938.110

Gold Scales
1849
Scales and weights: brass
Box: tin
Scales: 8½ × 8 × 2⅝ in.; 21.6 × 20.3 × 6.7 cm.
Box: 1¼ × 5½ × 3⅛ in.; 3.2 × 14 × 7.9 cm.
Gift of Charles B. Pike
1929.8abc

Landing of the American Forces Under Gen. Scott at Vera Cruz March 9th 1847
Color lithograph
Nathaniel Currier
1847
Ink on paper
10 × 14⅛ in.; 25.4 × 35.9 cm.
X.310
ICHi-22027

The Battle of Sacramento
Color lithograph
Nathaniel Currier
1847
Ink on paper
13⅛ × 18⅛ in.; 33.3 × 46.0 cm.
Gift of Stuyvesant Peabody
1955.289
ICHi-22028

Winfield Scott
Steel engraving after a painting by Alonzo Chappel
1858
Ink on paper
10⅜ 6⅝ in.; 26.3 × 16.8 cm.

Shako Plates
c. 1846
Brass
5 × 3⅛ in.; 12.7 × 7.9 cm. (average size)
Charles F. Gunther Collection
1920.9, 1920.14–1920.16, 1920.18, 1920.20

Chin Straps
1846
Brass, leather
6¾ × 1½ in.; 17.1 × 3.8 cm.
Charles F. Gunther Collection
1920.12–1920.13

.54 Caliber Flintlock Pistol
Simeon North
U.S. Model 1819; made 1821
Walnut, steel, brass
Length: 15½ in.; 39.4 cm.
X.1491

.64 Caliber Percussion Musket
Harper's Ferry Arsenal
U.S. Model 1833, made in 1839
Walnut, steel
Length: 43 in.; 109.2 cm.
Charles F. Gunther Collection
1920.1357

Cavalry Saber and Scabbard
Ames Manufacturing Company
U.S. Model 1840
Steel, brass, leather
Overall length: 41 in.; 104.1 cm.
Gift of Mary Merrilies
1926.119 ab

Shako Hat
c. 1846
Leather, brass, feather
23 × 6¼ × 9¼ in.; 58.4 × 15.9 × 23.5 cm.
Charles F. Gunther Collection
1920.38

Costumes Mexicains
Color lithograph
c. 1826
Ink on paper
11¼ × 9 in.; 28.6 × 22.9 cm.
1957.44
ICHi-22141

*Proclamation to the Mexicans from Major General
    Winfield Scott*
Broadside
April 11, 1847
Ink on paper
11⅝ × 9 in.; 29.5 × 22.9 cm.
ICHi-22136

*Resignation of the Mexican President, General
    Santa Anna*
Broadside
May 28, 1847
Ink on paper
11⅝ × 8⅞ in.; 29.5 × 22.5 cm.
ICHi-22137

Mexican Horse Bit
c. 1845
Plated silver
2 × 4⅜ × 20 in.; 5.1 × 11.1 × 50.8 cm.
Gift of Adolf B. and Orville E. Babcock
1937.10

Zachary Taylor
Daguerreotype
c. 1848
Glass plate, wood frame
9⅞ × 8¾ in.; 25.1 × 22.2 cm.
Charles F. Gunther Collection
ICHi-22139

John C. Calhoun
Painting
James R. Lambdin (1807–1889)
c. 1845
Oil on canvas
43¼ × 34¼ in.; 108.9 × 88.6 cm.
Charles F. Gunther Collection
1920.3

Portrait of Daniel Webster
Painting
c. 1845
Oil on canvas
29¾ × 25 in.; 75.6 × 63.5 cm.
Charles F. Gunther Collection
1920.1363

Portrait of Henry Clay
Painting
Attributed to Matthew H. Jouett
(1788–1827)
c. 1824
Oil on wood panel
29⅞ × 24½ in.; 75.9 × 62.2 cm.
1955.8

Henry Clay Addressing the Senate
Steel engraving
John M. Butler and Alfred Long
1854
Ink on paper
8 × 10⅛ in.; 20.3 × 25.7 cm.
ICHi-22205

Practical Illustration of the Fugitive Slave Law
Lithograph cartoon
E.C.
c. 1850
Ink on paper
14 × 7⅞ in.; 35.6 × 45.4 cm.
ICHi-22029

"Minutes of Meeting of the Committee for the
    Relief of the Fugitives in Canada"
Manuscript
November 11, 1850
Ink on paper
9⅞ × 7⅞ in.; 25.1 × 20 cm.
Zebina Eastman Collection

FOUR *THE IMPENDING CRISIS*

Political Chart of the United States
Broadside
Publisher: "Rocky Mountain Club"
1856
Ink on paper
13½ × 17¾ in.; 34.3 × 45.1 cm.
ICHi-22030

*Proceedings of the Republican State Convention,
    Held at Springfield, Illinois, June 16, 1858*
Pamphlet
Publisher: Bailhache & Baker, Springfield,
    Illinois
1858
Ink on paper
10½ × 8¾ in.; 26.7 × 22.2 cm.

Letter from Abraham Lincoln to Stephen A.
    Douglas concerning terms for the 1858 debate
Manuscript
Abraham Lincoln
July 31, 1858
Ink on paper
9¾ × 7¾ in.; 24.8 × 19.7 cm.
Bequest of Lambert Tree

Portrait of Stephen A. Douglas
Painting
Lussier
c. 1855
Oil on canvas
36⅝ × 28¼ in.; 93 × 71.8 cm.
X.104

Abraham Lincoln
Painting
Thomas Hicks (1823–1890)
1860
Oil on canvas
30½ × 25½ in.; 77.5 × 64.8 cm.
Bequest of Oscar B. Cintas
1959.212

Stephen A. Douglas
Photograph
Case & Getchell, Boston
c. 1860
Albumen print
4 × 2½ in.; 10.2 × 6.4 cm.
Gift of Frederick E. Olinger
ICHi-10097

Abraham Lincoln
Photograph
Attributed to C. S. German, Springfield, Illinois
1858
Albumen print
8⅛ × 6⅛ in.; 20.6 × 15.6 cm.
Charles F. Gunther Collection
ICHi-22206

The Little Giant in the Character of the Gladiator
Lithograph cartoon
1858
Ink on paper
15¾ × 11½ in.; 40 × 29.2 cm.
X.344
ICHi-22032

Letter from Stephen Douglas to August
    Belmont—"Nothing will do any good which
    does not take the slavery question out of
    Congress forever."
Manuscript
Stephen Douglas
December 25, 1860
Ink on paper
8⅛ × 10 in.; 20.6 × 25.4 cm.

Stephen Douglas
Sculpture
Leonard Volk (1828–1895)
1858–1860
Marble
26½ × 8 × 7 in.; 67.3 × 20.3 × 17.8 cm.
X.58

John Brown
Photograph
c. 1855
Albumen print
6⅞ × 5⅜ in.; 17.5 × 13.7 cm.
Gift of Edmund J. Blair
1957.38

*The Holy Bible, Containing the Old and New
    Testaments* (used by John Brown, with
    passages marked by him while in prison,
    Charleston, Virginia, 1859)
Book
Publisher: American Bible Society, New York
1854
Ink on paper with ink and pencil markings;
    leather binding
7⅛ × 9⅜ in.; 18.1 × 23.8 cm.
Gift of Frank G. Logan

Eyeglasses and Case (allegedly used by John
    Brown)
c. 1850
Glass, steel; leather case
Glasses: 3 × 2¾ in.; 7.6 × 7 cm.
Case: 1⅞ × 2⅝ in.; 4.8 × 6.7 cm.
Charles F. Gunther Collection
1920.31ab

.31 Caliber Percussion Revolver and Holster
    (allegedly used by John Brown in Kansas)
Massachusetts Arms Company, Chicopee Falls,
    Massachusetts
c. 1855
Steel, wood, leather
Pistol length: 12 in.; 30.5 cm.
Holster length: 14¾ in.; 37.5 cm.
Gift of Frank G. Logan
1917.52ab

Bowie Knife with Sheath (allegedly used by
    Owen Brown at Harper's Ferry)
M. H. Nicholson, Union St. Works, Sheffield,
    England
1840–1860
Steel, wood, brass, leather
13 × 2¼ in.; 33 × 5.7 cm.
Charles F. Gunther Collection
1920.77 ab

*Harper's Ferry Insurrection—Bringing the
    Prisoners out of the Engine House*
Wood engraving
Frank Leslie's Illustrated Newspaper
November 5, 1859
Ink on paper
6⅞ × 10¼ in.; 17.5 × 26 cm.

Pike for Slave Rebellion
Charles Blair (on contract to John Brown)
c. 1859
Wood, iron
79⅜ × 4⅜ × 1¼ in.; 201.6 × 11.1 × 3.2 cm.

John Brown's Last Note (written in prison,
    Charleston, Virginia)
Manuscript
John Brown
December 2, 1859
Ink on paper
3 × 7¾ in.; 7.6 × 19.7 cm.
Gift of Frank G. Logan

John Brown Commemorative Medals
J. Wurden, France
1859
Bronze
Diameter: 2¼ in.; 5.7 cm.
X.4ab

*John Brown Meeting the Slave mother and her
    Child on the steps of Charleston jail on his way
    to execution*
Color lithograph after a painting by Louis
    Ransom
Currier & Ives, New York
1863
Ink on paper
13⅞ × 9⅛ in.; 35.2 × 23.2 cm.
Charles F. Gunther Collection
ICHi-22033

John Brown Commemorative Ring
1859
Gold, glass, hair
1 × ¾ in.; 2.5 × 1.9 cm.
1917.2
Gift of Frank G. Logan

Abraham Lincoln
Photograph
Alexander Hesler, Chicago
June 3, 1860
Made from copy negative of original glass plate
8¾ × 6½ in.; 22.2 × 16.5 cm.
ICHi-22034

The National Republican Platform
Broadside
Publisher: Press & Tribune Office, Chicago
1860
Ink on paper
13½ × 8⅛ in.; 34.3 × 20.6 cm.
ICHi-22035

*Life & Public Services of Hon. Abraham Lincoln
    of Illinois & Hon. Hannibal Hamlin of Maine*
Pamphlet
Publisher: Thayer & Eldridge, Boston
1860
Ink on paper
7⅞ × 5 in.; 20 × 12.7 cm. (closed)
7⅞ × 10¼ in.; 20 × 26 cm. (open)

"For President, Stephen A. Douglas. Vice
    President, Herschel V. Johnson"
Banner
1860
Ink on linen
8⅛ × 13 in.; 20.6 × 33 cm.
ICHi-22036

The Railsplitter
Painting
c. 1860
Oil on canvas
108 × 78 in.; 274.3 × 198 cm.
Gift of Maibelle Heikes Justice
1917.15

Life Mask and Hands of Abraham Lincoln
Leonard W. Volk (1828–1895)
1860
Bronze
Mask: 9½ × 8¼ × 5½ in.; 24.1 × 21 × 14
    cm.
Left hand: 6½ × 4¼ × 3 in.; 16.5 × 10.8 ×
    7.6 cm.
Right hand: 5¾ × 5¼ × 3½ in.; 14.6 × 13 ×
    8.9 cm.
Gift of Jules Berchem
Mask: X.521
Hands: 1913.76ab

Bust of Abraham Lincoln
Sculpture
Leonard W. Volk (1828–1895)
1860
Painted plaster
21¼ × 10¾ × 10 in.; 54 × 27.3 × 25.4 cm.
Gift of Joseph M. Cudahy Memorial Fund
1953.129

Lincoln Campaign Rally in Springfield
Photograph
1860
Albumen print
9¼ × 11⅜ in.; 23.5 × 28.9 cm.
Gift of Clara Schneider Berger and her sisters

*Grand Procession of Wide Awakes at New York on
   the Evening of October 3, 1860*
Wood engraving
Harper's Weekly
October 13, 1860
Ink on paper
15⅜ × 20¾ in.; 39.1 × 52.7 cm.

Wide Awakes' Campaign Torch (used in the
   presidential campaign of Abraham Lincoln)
1860
Lamp: tin
Pole: wood
Overall length: 58 in.; 147.3 cm.
Lamp: 7 × 8 × 6½ in.; 17.8 × 20.3 × 16.5
   cm.

Wide Awakes' Campaign Banner (used in the
   presidential campaign of Abraham Lincoln)
1860
Paint on cotton
48 × 66 in.; 121.9 × 167.6 cm.
Gift of James M. Doubleday, Jr.
1973.181

Progressive Democracy—Prospect of a Smash Up
Lithograph cartoon
Currier & Ives, New York
1860
Ink on paper
13½ × 17⅞ in.; 34.3 × 45.4 cm.
ICHi-22040

Election Ticket, Republican Party—Lincoln and
   Hamlin
1860
Ink on paper
6½ × 2⅝ in.; 16.5 × 6.7 cm.

Election Ticket, Democratic Party—Douglas and
   Johnson
1860
Ink on paper
7⅞ × 2¾ in.; 20 × 7 cm.

Election Ticket, National Democratic Party—
   Breckenridge and Lane
1860
Ink on paper
2¾ × 2¼ in.; 7 × 5.7 cm.

Election Ticket, Union Party—Bell and Everett
1860
Ink on paper
4½ × 3¼ in.; 11.4 × 8.3 cm.

Campaign Banner for John Bell
1860
Ink on cotton
23½ × 35¾ in.; 59.7 × 90.8 cm.
X.788

Abraham Lincoln Campaign Ribbons
1860
Silk
a) 6¾ × 2½ in.; 17.1 × 6.4 cm.
b) 8¼ × 2 in.; 21 × 5.1 cm.

The Rail Splitter
Newspaper
Editor: Charles Leib, Chicago
July 21, 1860
Ink on paper
10⅞ × 14½ in.; 27.61 × 36.8 cm.

Abraham Lincoln Campaign Coins
1860
Brass, white metal
a) Diameter: 1⅛ in.; 2.9 cm.
b) Diameter: 1⅛ in.; 2.9 cm.
c) Diameter: 1 in.; 2.5 cm.

Top Hat (allegedly used by Abraham Lincoln)
George Hall, Springfield, Illinois
c. 1860
Beaver pelt
6½ × 11¾ in.; 16.5 × 29.8 cm.
Charles F. Gunther Collection
1920.379

Militia Flag of the Saluda Sentinels
Ladies of Saluda, South Carolina
c. 1860
Embroidered silk
36 × 36 in.; 91.4 × 91.4 cm.
Charles F. Gunther Collection
1920.1023

*Secession Meeting in Front of the Mills House,
   Meeting Street, Charleston, S.C.*
Wood engraving
Frank Leslie's Illustrated Newspaper
December 1, 1860
Ink on paper
9⅛ × 10½ in.; 23.2 × 26.7 cm.

Secession Cockade with Badge
1861
Ink on silk, brass
Rosette diameter: 2¼ in.; 5.7 cm.
Button diameter: ⅝ in.; 1.6 cm.
Badge: 4⅞ × 3⅞ in.; 12.4 × 9.8 cm.
Charles F. Gunther Collection
1920.1005

Secession Cockade
1861
Silk, brass
Diameter: 1½ in.; 3.8 cm.
Charles F. Gunther Collection
1920. 1725

Secession Cockade
1861
Silk, brass
Diameter: 2 in.; 5.1 cm.
Charles F. Gunther Collection

Secession Cockade
1861
Felt, brass
Diameter: 1¾ in.; 4.4 cm.
Charles F. Gunther Collection
1920.1004

Secession Cockade
1861
Silk, brass
Diameter: 2 in.; 5.1 cm.
Charles F. Gunther Collection
1920.1006

Voting Ticket from the Secession Convention,
   Charleston, South Carolina
1860
Ink on paper
4½ × 2¾ in.; 11.4 × 7 cm.

The Union Is Dissolved
Broadside
The Charleston Mercury
December 20, 1860
Ink on paper
22¾ × 12⅝ in.; 57.8 × 32.1 cm.
Gift of Dr. John M. Pillsbury
ICHi-22037

*Declaration of Independence of the State of South
   Carolina*
Broadside
Printer: Evans & Cogswell, Charleston, South
   Carolina
1860
Ink on paper
18¾ × 11⅛ in.; 47.6 × 28.3 cm.
ICHi-22038

Gavel (used by James L. Orr, Speaker of the
House of Representatives, South Carolina, at
the time of secession)
1860
Wood
2½ × 9¾ in.; 6.4 × 24.8 cm.
Gift of Dr. John M. Pillsbury
1923.83

Letter from Abraham Lincoln to Lyman
Trumbull Endorsing Compromise Efforts that
"do not touch the territorial question."
Manuscript
Abraham Lincoln
December 21, 1860
Ink on paper
7⅞ × 5¼ in.; 20 × 13.3 cm.
Gift of Foreman M. Lebold

Uncle Abe
Lithograph cartoon
Crehen, Richmond, Virginia
March 1861
Ink on paper
8¾ × 14 in.; 22.2 × 35.6 cm.
ICHi-22039

Portrait of Jefferson Davis
Painting
Christian F. Schwerdt
c. 1875
Oil on canvas
46 × 39⅛ in.; 116.8 × 99.4 cm.
Charles F. Gunther Collection
1920.175

Jefferson Davis's Cabinet Nominations
Manuscript
Jefferson Davis
February 21, 1861
Ink on paper
9⅞ × 7⅞ in.; 25.1 × 20 cm.

Alexander Stephens
Photograph
c. 1860
Albument print
10½ × 8⅛ in.; 26.7 × 20.6 cm.
ICHi-22140

Constitution of the Confederate States of America
Pamphlet
1861
Ink on paper
7¾ × 4⅞ in.; 19.7 × 12.4 cm. (closed)
7¾ × 9⅝ in.; 19.7 × 24.4 cm. (open)

Electrotype Copy of Seal of the Confederacy
1873
Brass
Diameter: 3¾ in.; 9.5 cm.
Charles F. Gunther Collection
1920.983

Electrotype Copy of Seal of the Confederate
Treasury Department
c. 1870
Copper
Diameter: 2 in.; 5.1 cm.
Charles F. Gunther Collection
1920.1079.3

Electroplate Copy of Seal of the Confederate
War Department
c. 1870
Copper
Diameter: 1⅞ in.; 4.8 cm.
Charles F. Gunther Collection
1920.1709.2

Electroplate Copy of Seal of the Confederate
Post Office Department
c. 1870
Copper
Diameter: 2⅛ in.; 5.4 cm.
Charles F. Gunther Collection
1920.1090

Confederate Stamp Plate
c. 1861
Copper
10¼ × 8⅝ in.; 26 × 21.9 cm.
Gift of Brother Joseph Schmidt
1933.230

"Perspective View of the Harbor & City of
Charleston"
Map
Jacob Weiss, Philadelphia
c. 1861
Ink on paper
10⅞ × 14 in.; 27.6 × 35.6 cm.

Telegrams from Leroy P. Walker to General
Braxton Bragg Reporting the attack on Ft.
Sumter
April 11, 12, and 16, 1861
Ink on paper
7½ × 5¾ in.; 19.1 × 14.6 cm.
Gift of Ralph A. Bard

*Bombardment of Fort Sumter, Charleston Harbor,
12th & 13th of April, 1861*
Color lithograph
Currier & Ives, New York
1861
Ink on paper
9⅞ × 13⅞ in.; 25.1 × 35.2 cm.
Gift of Charles B. Pike
ICHi-22041

The Battle of Fort Sumter!
Broadside
The Charleston Mercury
April 14, 1861
Ink on paper
15½ × 11¾ in.; 39.4 × 29.8 cm.
ICHi-22042

View of Ft. Sumter, South Carolina
Painting
J. Linton Chapman after sketches by Conrad
Wise Chapman
c. 1863
Oil on canvas
22½ × 31½ in.; 57.2 × 80 cm.
1957.612

FIVE *THE FIRST MODERN WAR*

First Official flag of the Confederate States of
America (attributed to the "Secessionist
Ladies" of Washington, D.C.)
1861
Cotton
53¾ × 77 in.; 136.5 × 195.6 cm.
Charles F. Gunther Collection
1920.1627

United States Flag with 34 Stars
Women employed by Cook & McClain's,
Chicago
1861
Wool, cotton
53 × 77½ in.; 134.6 × 196.9 cm.
Gift of Mrs. Richard Wharton
1944.145

19th Illinois Recruits
Recruitment broadside
J. Barnet, Chicago
1863
Ink on paper
24 × 18 in.; 61 × 45.7 cm.
ICHi-22043

Freemen, Rally
Recruitment broadside
April 18, 1861
Ink on paper
15¾ × 12½ in.; 40 × 31.8 cm.
Gift of the Estate of Mrs. Fred G. Mitchell
ICHi-22044

On to Richmond!
Recruitment broadside
Bay State Press, Lynn, Massachusetts
c. 1861
Ink on paper
33⅞ × 23⅞ in.; 86 × 60.6 cm.
ICHi-22045

Rally for the Massachusetts First Regiment
Recruitment broadside
Keenan's Card & Job Press
c. 1862
Ink on paper
25¾ × 19½ in.; 65.4 × 49.5 cm.
ICHi-22046

Volunteers Wanted! For Company M, Colonel Owen's 2d Regiment, Baker's Brigade!
Recruitment broadside
King & Baird, Printers, Philadelphia
1861
Ink on paper
32⅞ × 23⅜ in.; 83.5 × 60.6 cm.
ICHi-22130

Volunteers Wanted for Company A, Irish Brigade
Recruitment broadside
King & Baird, Printers, Philadelphia
1861
32⅝ × 22¼ in.; 82.9 × 56.5 cm.
ICHi-22131

Descriptive Roll of Company B, First Regiment, U.S. Artillery, Illinois Volunteers
Manuscript book
1861–1863
Ink on paper, leather binding
15⅝ × 21 in.; 39.7 × 53.3 cm. (open)
Gift of Henry A. Rumsey

9th Vermont Infantry Drum and Sticks
c. 1861
Wood, skin, rope, leather, brass
15½ × 16⅝ in.; 39.4 × 42.2 cm.
Charles F. Gunther Collection
1920.691

Flag of the Wee Tee Volunteers
1860
Embroidered silk
44 × 39½ in.; 111.8 × 100.3 cm.
Charles F. Gunther Collection
1920.1683

Flag of the Confederate Union District Volunteers
The Ladies of Unionville, South Carolina
1861
Painted silk
45 × 40 in.; 114.3 × 101.6 cm.
Charles F. Gunther Collection
1920.1024

U.S. Army Recruiting Service
Broadside
1862
Ink on paper
18⅞ × 12½ in.; 47.9 × 31.8 cm.
ICHi-22048

Recruiting in New York, August, 1861
Wood engraving
Harper's Weekly
September 7, 1861
Ink on paper
15¾ × 10¾ in.; 40 × 27.3 cm.

Departure of the 7th Regiment
Color lithograph
Sarony, Major, & Knapp
1861
Ink on paper
6¾ × 8⅝ in.; 17.1 × 21.9 cm.

Chicago Zouaves Cadets Drill Team, Utica, New York
Painting
J. Groff
c. 1860
Oil on panel
29 × 46¼ in.; 73.7 × 117.5 cm. (unframed)
1980.227

Mulligan's Brigade!
Recruitment broadside
1863
Ink on paper
21¾ × 16⅞ in.; 55.2 × 42.9 cm.
ICHi-22049

Presentation Sword and Scabbard of Colonel James A. Mulligan
1864
Steel, brass, wood, sharkskin
Length: 41½ in.; 105.4 cm.
Gift of Mrs. John C. Carroll
1939.207ab

Spitoon with Confederate Flag Motif
c. 1861
Ceramic
3¾ × 8¼ in.; 9.5 × 21 cm.
Charles F. Gunther Collection
1920.1727

Elmer Ellsworth Commemorative Pitcher
Millington & Astbury
1861
Ceramic
9⅜ × 6⅛ × 9⅛ in.; 23.8 × 15.6 × 23.2 cm.
1984.278

Union Patriotic Envelopes
Harbach & Bro., Philadelphia, and
 Wm. Ridenburgh, New York
c. 1861
Ink on paper
5½ × 3⅛ in.; 14 × 7.9 cm.

Six Military and Patriotic Illustrated Songs
Song book
Charles Magnus, New York
c. 1862
Ink on paper
ICHi-22099

"We'll Go Down Ourselves"
Sheet music
Henry C. Work
Publisher: Root & Cady, Chicago
1862
Ink on paper
14⅛ × 10¾ in.; 35.9 × 27.3 cm.

"When Johnny Comes Marching Home"
Sheet music
Louis Lambert
Publisher: Henry Tolman & Co., Boston
1863
Ink on paper
13 × 10⅛ in.; 33 × 25.7 cm.

"Battle Cry of Freedom"
Sheet music
George F. Root
Publisher: Root & Cady, Chicago
1862
Ink on paper
13⅛ × 10 in.; 33.3 × 25.4 cm.

"Marching Through Georgia"
Sheet Music
Henry Clay Work
Publisher: Root & Cady, Chicago
1865
Ink on paper
13½ × 10¼ in.; 34.3 × 26 cm. (closed)
13½ × 20½ in.; 34.3 × 52.1 cm. (open)

"I Wish I Was in Dixie's Land"
Sheet music
Jean Manns
Publisher: Firth, Pond & Co., New York
1860
Ink on paper
13 × 10¼ in.; 33 × 26 cm.

"God Save the Southern Land"
Sheet music
Chaplin Cameron, C.S.A.
Publisher: George Dunn & Co., Richmond, Virginia
1864
Ink on paper
12 × 9½ in.; 30.5 × 24.1 cm.

"General Stonewall Jackson"
Sheet music
Publisher: A. E. Blackmar, New Orleans
1865
Ink on paper
14 × 10¾ in.; 35.6 × 27.3 cm.

"The Bonnie Blue Flag"
Sheet music
1861
Ink on paper
11¾ × 10 in.; 29.8 × 25.4 cm.

Confederate Flag
Women of Richmond, Virginia
c. 1861
Wood, wire, paper, ribbon
24 × 39¼ × 1 in.; 61 × 99.7 × 2.5 cm.
Charles F. Gunther Collection
1920.1688

Rebel Gunpowder—Notice to the Ladies of Selma
Broadside
1863
Ink on paper
7¾ × 3⅞ in.; 19.7 × 9.8 cm.
ICHi-22104

Confederate Patriotic Envelopes
c. 1861
Ink on paper
3¼ × 5⅜ in.; 8.3 × 13.7 cm.

U.S. Army Fatigue Jacket
John Martin, New York
c. 1862
Wool
23 × 17½ in.; 58.4 × 44.6 cm.
Sleeve length: 26½ in.; 67.3 cm.

Pair of Soldier's Shoes
1861–1865
Leather, wood, brass, iron
4¾ × 3⅝ × 9½ in.; 12.1 × 9.2 × 24.1 cm.
X.405ab

U.S. Army Pup Tent—one-half
1861–1865
Canvas
63 × 60 in.; 160 × 152.4 cm.

Camp Scene on the Pamunky River
Photograph
Publisher: Taylor and Huntington, Hartford, Connecticut
1862
Albumen print
9 × 11 in.; 22.9 × 27.9 cm.
ICHi-22156

Camp
Photograph
c. 1863
Albumen print
8½ × 11 in.; 21.6 × 27.9 cm.
ICHi-22157

Zouave Badge
c. 1856
Gold, silk
2⅜ × 1⅜ in.; 6 × 3.5 cm.

Infantry Drum (used by James Harvey McCormick, musician, 147th Regiment, Illinois Infantry)
1861–
Painted wood
11⅛ × 16⅛ in.; 28.3 × 41 cm.
Gift of David H. McCormick
1985.308

Artillery Bugle (used by Everett H. Rexford, Bugler for Battery A, Chicago Light Artillery)
1861–1865
Copper, brass
7⅜ × 15⅜ × 5⅜ in.; 18.7 × 39.1 × 13.7 cm.
Gift of Mrs. George Pettijohn
1950.111b

Soldier's Sewing Kit
1861–1865
Leather, silk, felt, cotton, brass, steel, bone
9¼ × 15⅝ in.; 23.5 × 39.7 cm.
XA-2039

Canteen
1861–1865
Canvas, tin
30 × 8¼ × 3¼ in.; 76.2 × 21 × 8.3 cm.
XA-2082

Assorted Soldier's Eating Utensils
1861–1865
Silver, steel, tin, bone, wood
10 in.; 25.4 cm. (average size)

Razor, Razor Strop
Razor and case: Frederick Reynolds Sheffield
Razor strop: J. R. Torrey & Co., Worcester, Massachusetts
1861–1865
Metal, tortoise shell, cardboard, leather, wood
Razor strop: 1⅝ × 12⅞ × 1⅝ in.; 4.1 × 32.7 × 4.1 cm.
1976.74.32a–f

Gameboard and Dice
1861–1865
Wood, bone
Box: 6⅜ × 3⅜ × 2½ in.; 16.2 × 8.6 × 6.4 cm.
Dice: ½ in.; 1.3 cm.
1976.74.5abc

Coffee Pot
1861–1865
Tin
Height: 9¾ in.; 24.8 cm.
Base diameter: 7⅛ in.; 18.1 cm.
1976.74.9

Camp Cooking Stove
1861–1865
Tin
8 × 8½ in.; 20.3 × 21.6 cm.
1976.74.12abcd

Playing Cards
a) Goodall & Son, London
b) Samuel Hart & Co., Philadelphia
1861–
Paper
a) 3⅝ × 2½ in.; 9.2 × 6.4 cm.
b) 3½ × 2½ in.; 8.9 × 6.4 cm.
b) Albert Dickinson Civil War Collection
a) XA-182
b) 1920.1099

Chewing Tobacco
1861–1865
J. W. Loomis, Suffield, Connecticut
Tobacco, paper
3⅝ × 2⅛ × ⅝ in.; 9.2 × 5.4 × 1.6 cm.
1976.74.19

Food Container
1861–1865
Tin
4 × 5¼ in.; 10.2 × 13.3 cm.
1976.74.7a

Folding Gameboard for Checkers and Backgammon
1861–1865
Wood
15⅜ × 7½ × ⅜ in.; 39.1 × 19.1 × 1 cm.
Gift of Mr. Thomas A. Larsen
1928.57

Dominoes
1861–1865
Ivory, wood
Ivory: 1½ × ¾ × ¼ in.; 3.8 × 1.9 × 0.6 cm.
Wood: 1¾ × ¾ × ¼ in.; 4.4 × 1.9 × 0.6 cm.
1976.74.6

Folding Camp Chair
1861–1865
Wood and metal frame; wool tapestry seat
31½ × 16 × 17 in.; 80 × 40.6 × 43.2 cm.
Charles F. Gunther Collection
1920.881

Quartermaster's Trunk (used by Colonel Henry
  Howland)
1861–1865
Pine
16 × 32⅝ × 17¾ in.; 40.6 × 82.9 × 45.1
  cm.
Gift of Mr. and Mrs. F. Gale Walker, Jr.
1985.330.1

Rules of Quartermaster's Barracks
Broadside
1865
Ink on paper
10⅝ × 13½ in.; 27 × 34.3 cm.
Gift of Mr. and Mrs. Gale Walker, Jr.
1985.330

Colonel Henry Howland
Photograph
c. 1865
Albumen print
10 × 8 in.; 25.4 × 20.3 cm.
Gift of Mr. and Mrs. F. Gale Walker, Jr.
1985.330
ICHi-22151

Quartermaster's Account Book
Manuscript book
William H. Bailhache
July–December 1862
Ink on paper
15⅝ × 9¾ in.; 39.7 × 24.8 cm. (closed)
15⅝ × 19½ in.; 39.7 × 49.5 cm. (open)

Field Press
Lowe Press Co., Boston
1861–1865
Iron, felt, wood
37½ × 16 × 11½ in.; 95.3 × 40.6 × 29.2
  cm.
Charles F. Gunther Collection

*The War Eagle & Camp Journal of the Army of
  West*
Soldiers' newspaper
Editor: Reverend N. Shumate
Publisher: C. H. James, D. G. Scouten
January 1, 1862
Ink on paper
11¾ × 12 in.; 29.8 × 30.5 cm.

The New Testament (carried through the war by
  S. C. Stevens [?], Chicago Board of Trade
  Battery)
Book
Publisher: American Bible Society, New York
1860
Ink on paper, leather binding
3¾ × 2½ × 1 in.; 9.5 × 6.4 × 2.5 cm.
  (closed)

Diary of Silas S. Huntley, Sergeant in Company
  I, 37th Regiment, New York State Volunteers
January 1, 1862–December 31, 1862
Ink on paper; leather binding
6⅛ × 4 × ½ in.; 15.6 × 10.2 × 1.3 cm.
Gift of Mrs. Huntley H. Gilbert

Pepper Container
1861–1865
Wood
1¼ × 2½ × ⅝ in.; 3.2 × 6.4 × 1.6 cm.
XA-2213

Pocket Knife
1861–1865
Bone, steel
2¾ × 1 × ½ in.; 7 × 2.5 × 1.3 cm.

Shaving Mirror (used by James W. Eldridge,
  U.S. Army)
1861–1865
Glass, wood
6⅞ × 4¾ × ⅞ in.; 17.5 × 12.1 × 2.2 cm.

Matches
1861–1865
Wood
2½ × 1⅞ in.; 6.4 × 4.8 cm.

Skillet
1861–1865
Tin
2 × 8¾ × 6¾ in.; 5.1 × 22.2 × 17.1 cm.

Case
1861–1865
Tin
4¼ × 7¼ × 1⅞ in.; 10.8 × 18.4 × 4.8 cm.
1976.74.13

Soldier's Carrying Case with Knife and Pencil
1861–1865
Leather; bone, steel; wood, lead
Case: 3⅞ × 2⅜ × ½ in.; 9.8 × 6 × 1.3 cm.
Knife length: 3⅛ in.; 7.9 cm.
Pencil length: 2¾ in.; 7 cm.

Toothbrush (marked "J.R.W. 9th R.I.V.")
1862
Wood, shell, bristle
Length: 4¼ in.; 10.8 cm. (partially open)
Gift of Mrs. Dewey Ericsson
1955.192

Cup
1861–1865
Tin
3½ × 3¼ in.; 8.9 × 8.3 cm.

Officer's Frock Coat and Cap (used by John R.
  Winterbotham, 1st Lieutenant and Adjutant of
  the 155th New York Infantry)
Coat: Brooks Brothers, New York
Cap: Jas. Y. Davis, Washington, D.C.
1862–1864
Coat: serge, velvet, brass buttons
Cap: serge, braid, brass, leather
Coat: 41 × 16 in.; 104.1 × 40.6 cm.
Sleeve length: 24 in.; 61 cm.
Gift of John R. Winterbotham, Jr.
1938.130ac

General Joe Hooker and Staff, June 1863
Photograph
Publisher: Taylor & Huntington, Hartford,
  Connecticut
1863
Albumen print
9 × 11⅛ in.; 22.9 × 28.3 cm.
ICHi-22061

*General Caldwell and Staff, at Fair Oaks, June
  1862*
Photograph
Barnard & Gibson
1862
Albumen print
4½ × 6 in.; 11.4 × 15.2 cm.
ICHi-22062

General F. P. Blair and Staff
Photograph
Publisher: Taylor & Huntington, Hartford,
  Connecticut
c. 1862
Albumen print
9 × 11 in.; 22.9 × 27.9 cm.
ICHi-22063

General Rufus Ingalls and Staff
Photograph
Publisher: Taylor & Huntington, Hartford,
  Connecticut
c. 1862
Albumen print
9 × 11 in.; 22.9 × 27.9 cm.
ICHi-22064

Sutler's Coupons
1861–1865
Ink on paper
a–b) 2¾ × 4½ in.; 7 × 11.4 cm.
c) 2½ × 3¾ in.; 6.4 × 9.5 cm.
d) 2⅝ × 6⅜ in.; 6.7 × 16.2 cm.

The Sutler's Tent
Photograph
c. 1862
Albumen print
9 × 11 in.; 22.9 × 27.9 cm.
ICHi-22216

Dirk
Joseph Mappin & Brothers
c. 1850
Steel, ivory
9¼ × 1⅞ × ¾ in.; 23.5 × 4.8 × 1.9 cm.
Gift of Mrs. Francis E. Manierre
1959.255

Dirk with Sheath
c. 1820
Steel, wood, leather
9⅛ × 1⅞ in.; 23.2 × 5.8 cm.
Charles F. Gunther Collection
XA.252
1920.1549b

Come and Join Us Brothers
Color lithograph
Publisher: The Supervisory Committee for
    Recruiting Colored Regiments, Philadelphia
Printer: P. S. Duval & Son, Philadelphia
c. 1863
Ink on paper
13¾ × 17⅞ in.; 34.9 × 45.4 cm.
Charles F. Gunther Collection
ICHi-22051

*Letter from Abraham Lincoln to U.S. Grant
    Regarding the "raising of colored troops"*
Manuscript
Abraham Lincoln
August 9, 1863
Ink on paper
9¾ × 8⅞ in.; 24.8 × 22.5 cm.
The Lincoln Collection

22nd Regiment U.S. Colored Troops/Company E
Broadside with company roll call and
    illustrations
c. 1865
Ink on paper
19⅞ × 16 in.; 50.5 × 40.6 cm.
ICHi-22052

*Guerre d'Amérique—Volontaires nègres venant
    s'enrôler dans le corps d'armée du général Grant*
(American war—negro volunteers coming to
    enroll in General Grant's Army Corps)
Wood engraving
C. Maurand
Le Monde Illustré
c. 1863
Ink on paper
9⅛ × 12⅛ in.; 23.2 × 30.8 cm.
ICHi-22053

*Battery A, 2nd U.S. Colored Artillery (Light)—
    Department of the Cumberland*
Photograph
c. 1863
Albumen print
8 × 10 in.; 20.3 × 25.4 cm.
ICHi-22054

Company "E"—4th U.S. Colored Infantry
Photograph
Publisher: Taylor & Huntingdon, Hartford,
    Connecticut
c. 1863
Albumen print
9 × 11 in.; 22.9 × 27.9 cm.
ICHi-22055

Attack on Ft. Wagner
Steel engraving after a painting by Thomas Nast
Johnson, Fry & Co., New York
1867
Ink on paper
7¼ × 10½ in.; 18.4 × 26.7 cm.
ICHi-22046

The Massacre at Fort Pillow
Wood engraving
Harper's Weekly
April 30, 1864
Ink on paper
10½ × 15⅞ in.; 26.7 × 40.3 cm.

*Statement of Corporal Frank Hogan on the Fort
    Pillow Massacre*
Manuscript
Frank Hogan, Corporal in Company A, 6th U.S.
    Heavy Artillery
April 30, 1864
Ink on paper
9½ × 7⅜ in.; 24.1 × 18.7 cm.

Unidentified Black Soldiers, U.S. Army
c. 1863
Tintypes
8 × 10 in.; 20.3 × 25.4 cm. (average size)
ICHi-22166-22172, 22194, 22195, 22217

Battle of Gettysburg, July 3rd, 1863
Painting
Paul D. Philippoteaux (1846–?)
1880
Oil on canvas
47¾ × 113½ in.; 121.3 × 288.3 cm. (2 panels)
Charles F. Gunther Collection
1920.190ab

*Battle of the Iron-clads "Monitor" and
    "Merrimac," March 9th, 1862*
Painting
William Torgerson (?–c. 1890)
1877
Oil on canvas
35¾ × 55¾ in.; 90.8 × 141.6 cm.
Gift of Mrs. Eleanore Rang
1910.1

View of the Arsenal Yard, Washington, D.C.
Photograph
c. 1862
Albumen print
9⅛ × 12¾ in.; 23.2 × 32.4 cm.
ICHi-22065

(Fort Richardson, Va.) Camp 1st Conn. Artillery
Photograph
Matthew B. Brady
1861
Albumen print
14⅝ × 16½ in.; 37.1 × 41.9 cm.
Gift of Marshall Field, Jr.
ICHi-22067

*The "Lincoln Gun" at Fortress Monroe, Va.,
    December 3, 1864*
Photograph
Publisher: Taylor & Huntingdon, Hartford,
    Connecticut
1864
Albumen print
9 × 11⅛ in.; 22.9 × 28.3 cm.
ICHi-22066

Thirteen-inch Mortar "Dictator"
Photograph
Alexander Gardner
Publisher: Taylor & Huntington, Hartford,
    Connecticut
1864
Albumen print
9 × 11 in.; 22.9 × 27.9 cm.
ICHi-22068

Ruins of the Depot, Manassas Junction
Photograph
Matthew B. Brady
1862
Albumen print
15⅞ × 19⅞ in.; 40.3 × 50.5 cm.
ICHi-22070

Telegraph Office in the Field
Photograph
Alexander Gardner
Publisher: Taylor & Huntington, Hartford,
    Connecticut
1864
Albumen print
9 × 11 in.; 22.9 × 27.9 cm.
ICHi-22071

*.58 Caliber Percussion Rifle-Musket with
    Angular Socket Bayonet*
National Armory, Springfield, Massachusetts
U.S. Model 1861, made in 1864
Walnut, steel
Rifle length: 56 in.; 142.2 cm.
Bayonet length: 21 × 2⅝ in.; 53.3 × 6.7 cm.
Charles F. Gunther Collection
1920.1386; 1920.1494

.60 Caliber Smooth-Bore Musket and Bayonet
Eli Whitney, Jr.
Model 1816, made in 1839
Brass, steel, walnut
Overall length: 57½ in.; 146.1 cm.
Charles F. Gunther Collection
1920.1379, 1920.1489

Smooth-Bore Musket
National Armory, Harper's Ferry, Virginia
1835
Walnut, steel
Length: 57 in.; 144.8 cm.
Charles F. Gunther Collection
1920.1470

.69 Caliber Smooth-Bore Percussion Musket
National Armory, Harper's Ferry Arsenal,
    Virginia
U.S. Model 1842, made in 1851
Walnut, steel, brass
Length: 57½ in.; 146.1 cm.
Charles F. Gunther Collection
1920.1453

.58 Caliber Percussion Rifle
National Armory, Harper's Ferry, Virginia
U.S. Model 1855, made in 1858
Walnut, steel
Length: 49 in.; 124.5 cm.
Gift of Mr. Elmer P. Renstrom, Jr.
1955.102

.52 Caliber Breech-Loading Carbine
Sharps Rifle Manufacturing Company, Hartford,
    Connecticut
1863
Walnut, steel, brass
Length: 47 in.; 119.4 cm.
Gift of Charles R. Walgreen, Jr.
1969.350

.54 Caliber Breech-Loading Carbine
Joslyn Firearms Company
c. 1864
Walnut, steel
Length: 37¾ in.; 95.9 cm.
Charles F. Gunther Collection
1920.1351

.54 Caliber Breech-Loading Carbine
Starr Arms Company, Yonkers, New York
1858
Walnut, steel, brass
Length: 38 in.; 96.5 cm.
Charles F. Gunther Collection
1920.396

.52 Caliber Percussion Rifle
Sharps Rifle Manufacturing Company
1863
Steel, walnut
Length: 46⅝ in.; 118.4 cm.
Gift of Charles R. Walgreen, Jr.
1969.350

Cartridge Box for 10 Cartridges for Sharp's .52
    Caliber Rifle
Sharp's Rifle Manufacturing Company, Hartford,
    Connecticut
c. 1862
Paper
2½ × 3 × 1¼ in.; 5.7 × 7.6 × 3.2 cm.
1976.74.34

.52 Caliber Percussion Carbine
Edward Gwyn and Abner C. Campbell
c. 1863
Walnut, steel
Length: 39 in.; 99.1 cm.
Gift of Charles R. Walgreen, Jr.
1969.196

.54 Caliber Breech-Loading Percussion Carbine
Burnside Rifle Company, Providence, Rhode
    Island
1864
Walnut, steel
Length: 39¼ in.; 99.7 cm.
Gift of Charles R. Walgreen, Jr.
1969.199

Cartridges for the Burnside Carbine
Burnside Rifle Company, Providence, Rhode
    Island
Patented 1856
Brass
Length: 2⅜ in.; 6 cm.

Cartridge Wrapper
Burnside Rifle Company, Providence, Rhode
    Island
c. 1864
Paper
2⅝ × 2½ × 1¼ in.; 6.7 × 6.4 × 3.2 cm.

.52 Caliber Repeating Carbine
Spencer Arms Company, Boston
1865
Walnut, steel
Length: 34½ in.; 87.6 cm.
Gift of Charles R. Walgreen, Jr.
1969.194

Cartridge Tube for the Spencer Repeating
    Carbine
Spencer Arms Company, Boston
1865
Steel
Length: 14½ in.; 36.8 cm.
Gift of Charles R. Walgreen, Jr.
1969.194

Cartridges for the Spencer Repeating Carbine
c. 1865
Copper, lead
1⅝ × ⅝ in. diameter; 4.1 × 1.6 cm. diameter

Cartridge Box
Paper
1¾ × 2⅞ × 1¼ in.; 4.4 × 7.3 × 3.2 cm.

Cartridge Box
E. Gaylord, Chicopee, Massachusetts
1864
Leather
12¼ × 3⅞ × 3 in.; 31.1 × 9.8 × 7.6 cm.
Charles F. Gunther Collection
1920.1728

.36 Caliber Percussion Revolver
Starr Arms Company, New York
Patented 1856
Steel, wood
12 × 5½ in.; 30.5 × 14 cm.
Gift of Mrs. Stella Bloss Norland
1937.16

.36 Caliber Percussion Revolver
Manhatten Fire Arms Company, Newark, New
    Jersey
Patented 1859
Steel, wood
11½ × 4⅝ in.; 29.2 × 11.7 cm.
Gift of Mrs. Hazel McKenna
1982.121.1

.31 Caliber Percussion Revolver
Springfield Arms Company
1851
Walnut, steel
Length: 11 in.; 27.9 cm.
Charles F. Gunther Collection
1920.406

Mountain Howitzer
U.S. Model 1841, made in 1861
Cyrus Alger & Company, Boston
Brass, wooden carriage
37 × 38 × 72 in.; 93.9 × 96.5 × 182.9 cm.

Noncommissioned Officer's Sword and Scabbard
Ames Manufacturing Company, Chicopee,
    Massachusetts
c. 1860
Steel, brass; leather
Length: 38¾ in.; 98.4 cm.

Bullet Mold
Massachusetts Arms Company
c. 1863
Brass
¾ × 5 × 1⅛ in.; 1.9 × 12.7 × 2.9 cm.
Charles F. Gunther Collection
1920.449

Noncommissioned Officer's Sword and Scabbard
Ames Manufacturing Company, Chicopee,
    Massachusetts
c. 1860
Steel, brass; leather, brass
Overall length: 38¾ in.; 98.4 cm.

Foot Officer's Sword and Scabbard (inscribed
    "Wm. W. Smith, Chicago, July 4th, 1861)
Ames Manufacturing Company, Chicopee,
    Massachusetts
c. 1861
Steel, brass; leather, sharkskin
Overall length: 37⅛ in.; 94.3 cm.
Charles F. Gunther Collection
1920.957

Confederate Sword
Confederate States of America
c. 1861
Iron, steel, wood
Length: 39¼ in.; 99.7 cm.
Charles F. Gunther Collection
1920.825

Confederate Officers Sword and Scabbard
    (inscribed "Franklin Buchanan, CSN")
Ames Manufacturing Company, Chicopee,
    Massachusetts
c. 1861
Steel, brass; leather, brass
Overall length: 35½ in.; 90.2 cm.
Charles F. Gunther Collection
1920.202ab

Presentation Sword and Scabbard (inscribed
    "Presented to Col. B. J. Sweet")
1864
Steel, brass; steel
Overall length: 39¼ in.; 99.7 cm.
Gift of the Estate of Mrs. Winifred B. Bonfils
1937.142ab

Field Glasses
James W. Queen, Philadelphia
c. 1861
Brass, leather, glass
6½ × 5½ × 2½ in.; 16.5 × 14 × 6.4 cm.
Gift of Mrs. Joseph M. Cudahy
1952.240ab

.58 Caliber Rifle-Musket with Maynard Tape
    Primer
National Armory, Harper's Ferry, Virginia
U.S. Model 1855, made in 1858
Walnut, steel
Length: 56 in.; 142.2 cm.
Charles F. Gunther Collection
1920.1077

"Historical and Military Map of the Border and
    Southern States"
Map with guide
Phelps and Watson, New York
1863
Ink on paper
25⅛ × 36¼ in.; 63.8 × 92.1 cm.

Drum (inscribed "Bull Run, Ft. Don'lson,
    Mana's J., Fair Oaks, Antietam")
c. 1862
Wood, skin, rope, leather
14 × 16¾ in.; 35.6 × 42.5 cm.

Battle of Bull Run, July 21, 1861
Wood engraving
C. Petit
Le Monde Illustré
c. 1861
Ink on paper
10⅛ × 13⅜ in.; 25.7 × 34 cm.
1956.413
ICHi-22134

Thomas J. (Stonewall) Jackson
Steel engraving
O'Neill, New York
c. 1863
Ink on paper
8⅞ × 5¾ in.; 22.5 × 14.6 cm.
ICHi-22133

General Grant at Fort Donelson
Painting
Paul D. Philippoteaux (1846–?)
c. 1870
Oil on canvas
18⅛ × 25½ in.; 46 × 64.8 cm.
Charles F. Gunther Collection
1920.1645

Victory!—Fort Donelson Is Ours
Broadside
The Union Advocate
February 18, 1862
Ink on paper
10⅛ × 5 in.; 25.7 × 12.7 cm.
ICHi-22138

*A Part of the Battle of Shiloh, Fought on the
    Morning of April 6th, 1862*
Lithograph based on a drawing by Wm. F.
    Mann, Company G, 13th Louisiana Volunteers
Lithographer: Max Rosenthal
Printers: L.N. Rosenthal, Philadelphia
c. 1862
14 × 17¾ in.; 35.5 × 45 cm.
Charles F. Gunther Collection
ICHi-22135

Battle Flag of the 13th Louisiana Volunteer
    Infantry
c. 1862
Wool, cotton
30½ × 55½ in.; 77.5 × 141 cm.
Charles F. Gunther Collection
1920.1685

Letter from J. R. Zearing to His Wife
    Describing the Battle of Shiloh
J. R. Zearing
April 8, 1862
Ink on paper
12¾ × 7¾ in.; 31.4 × 19.7 cm.

Grant in the Field
Photograph
Timothy H. O'Sullivan
May 6, 1864
Albumen print
6½ × 4¼ in.; 16.5 × 10.8 cm.
ICHi-22058

*Lieut. Gen. Grant and Chief of Staff, Gen.
    Rawlins, at his Head Quarters at Cold Harbor,
    Va.*
Stereocard
Brady & Co., Washington, D.C.
Publisher: E. & H. T. Anthony & Co., New
    York
1864
Albumen print
3¼ × 6⅞ in.; 8.3 × 17.5 cm.
Gift of Mrs. J. Rockefeller Prentice
ICHi-22049

Saddle with Leader, Bit, Bridle, and Reins
    (allegedly used by General U. S. Grant in the
    Civil War)
1861–1865
Leather, brass, hemp, white metal, wood
Saddle: 31 × 22 × 27 in.; 78.7 × 55.9 ×
    68.8 cm.
Leader: 41 × 1 × ½ in.; 104.1 × 2.5 × 1.3
    cm.
Bridle and reins: 59 × 3 × 5½ in.; 149.9 ×
    7.6 × 14 cm.
Gift of Hempstead Washburne
1897.15abc

Ulysses S. Grant
Painting
George P. A. Healy (1813–1894)
1868
Oil on canvas
18¾ × 14¾ in.; 47.6 × 37.5 cm.
Gift of Ezra B. McCagg
1896.9

Field Order from General Ulysses S. Grant to
    General Francis Jay Herron
Manuscript
Ulysses S. Grant
June 22, 1863
Ink on paper
4⅛ × 7⅞ in.; 10.5 × 20 cm.
Charles F. Gunther Collection

Albert Sidney Johnston
Steel engraving
H. B. Hall's Sons, New York
c. 1863
Ink on paper
9¼ × 6⅛ in.; 23.5 × 15.6 cm.
ICHi-22149

"Map of the Approaches to New Orleans"
Map
Bowen & Company, Philadelphia
c. 1862
Ink on paper
15 × 12 in.; 38.1 × 30.5 cm.

D. G. Farragut
Steel engraving
W. J. Jackman, after a photograph by
    J. Gurney & Son
Printer: Rich. Rutter & Co.
1865
Ink on paper
10⅛ × 6¼ in.; 25.7 × 15.9 cm.
Gift of the Kenneth Sawyer Goodman
    Foundation
ICHi-22143

Quadrant (from the U.S.S. *Hartford*)
E. & G. W. Blunt, New York
c. 1862
Brass, glass
8⅝ × 29⅝ × 1 in.; 21.9 × 75.2 × 2.5 cm.
Charles F. Gunther Collection

Gangway Board (from the U.S.S. *Hartford*)
c. 1862
Carved walnut
41 × 26½ × 2¾ in.; 104.1 × 67.3 × 7 cm.
Charles F. Gunther Collection
1920.1078

*Farragut's Fleet Passing Fort Jackson and Fort St.
    Philip, Louisiana, April 24, 1862*
Painting
J. Joffray
c. 1862
Oil on canvas
32¼ × 39⅛ in.; 81.9 × 99.4 cm.
Bequest of Mrs. Lewis L. Coburn
1932.27

"Order from Flag Officer David G. Farragut to
    Captain T. Baily Concerning the Order of
    Ships for the Attack on Fort St. Philip"
Manuscript
David G. Farragut
April 17, 1862
Ink on paper
12½ × 7⅞ in.; 31.8 × 20 cm.
David G. Farragut Collection

George B. McClellan
Photograph
c. 1862
Albumen print
6⅝ × 4⅜ in.; 16.8 × 11.1 cm.
Gift of Isabelle M. O'Brien
ICHi-22060

"Map of the Battlefield of Antietam"
Map
Lieutenant Wm. H. Willcox
P. S. Duval & Son, Philadelphia
c. 1862
Ink on paper
23¾ × 18½ in.; 60.3 × 47 cm.

The Battle of Sharpsburg, Md. Sept. 16th, 1862
Color lithograph
Currier & Ives, New York
1862
Ink on paper
12 × 15⅞ in.; 30.5 × 40.3 cm.
ICHi-22072

Ditch on the Right Wing
Photograph
Alexander Gardner
1862
Albumen print
4½ × 6 in.; 11.4 × 15.2 cm.
ICHi-22074

Completely Silenced
Photograph
Alexander Gardner
1862
Albumen print
4½ × 6 in.; 11.4 × 15.2 cm.
ICHi-22073

Letter from James L. Converse to His Wife
    Describing the Battle of Antietam
Manuscript
James L. Converse
September 30, 1862
Ink on paper
12⅜ × 7¾ in.; 31.4 × 19.7 cm.
Gift of Mrs. George McGhie.

"Gettysburg and Vicinity"
Map
Virtue & Yorston, New York
1864
Ink on paper
11¼ × 8⅜ in.; 28.6 × 21.3 cm.

Robert E. Lee
Photograph
Vannerson & Jones, Richmond, Virginia
c. 1863
Albumen Print
10⅛ × 8 in.; 25.7 × 20.3 cm.
ICHi-22057

General George Meade
Photograph
c. 1863
Albumen print
7¾ × 10½ in.; 19.7 × 26.7 cm.
ICHi-22145

Letter from Robert E. Lee to Jefferson Davis
    Reporting on Gettysburg
Manuscript
July 4, 1863
Robert E. Lee
Ink on paper
12½ × 8 in.; 31.8 × 20.3 cm.
Charles F. Gunther Collection

The Battle of Gettysburg
Color lithograph
Publisher: Thomas Kelly, New York
Printer: William C. Robertson
c. 1863
Ink on paper
21⅞ × 27¾ in.; 55.6 × 70.5 cm.
ICHi-22075

Dead Rebel Sharpshooter at Gettysburg
Photograph
Negative by Alexander Gardner and Timothy
    O'Sullivan
Timothy H. O'Sullivan
Publisher: Taylor & Huntington, Hartford,
    Connecticut
July 4–6, 1863
Albumen print
9 × 11 in.; 22.9 × 27.9 cm.
ICHi-22076

Union Dead on the Field of Gettysburg
Photograph
Timothy H. O'Sullivan
Publisher: Taylor & Huntington, Hartford,
    Connecticut
July 4–6, 1863
Albumen print
9 × 11 in.; 22.9 × 27.9 cm.
ICHi-22077

Union Dead on the Battlefield of Gettysburg
Photograph
Timothy H. O'Sullivan
Publisher: Taylor & Huntington, Hartford,
    Connecticut
July 4–6, 1863
Albumen print
9 × 11 in.; 22.9 × 27.9 cm.
ICHi-22078

Admiral Porter's Fleet Running the Rebel Blockade
*   of the Mississippi at Vicksburg, April 16th, 1863*
Color lithograph
Currier & Ives, New York
1863
Ink on paper
10 × 13⅞ in.; 25.4 × 35.2 cm.
Stuyvesant Peabody Memorial Collection
1963.13
ICHi-22132

Admiral D. D. Porter
Photograph
c. 1864
Albumen print
9 × 11 in.; 22.9 × 27.9 cm.
ICHi-22150

J. C. Pemberton
Steel engraving
H. B. Hall's Sons, New York
c. 1863
Ink on paper
9¼ × 6 in.; 23.5 × 15.2 cm.
Gift of A. A. Sprague
ICHi-22148

General John A. Logan's Headquarters at
*   Vicksburg*
Photograph
1863
Albumen print
7 × 9¼ in.; 17.8 × 23.5 cm.
ICHi-22079

Letter from Ulysses S. Grant to Lieutenant
    General J. C. Pemberton stating the terms for
    the surrender of Vicksburg
Manuscript
Ulysses S. Grant
July 3, 1863
Ink on paper
9⅞ × 7⅞ in.; 25.1 × 20 cm.
Charles F. Gunther Collection

Battle of the Wilderness, Attack at Spottsylvania
*   Court House*
Painting
Alonzo Chappel (1828–1887)
1865
Oil on canvas
18½ × 23½ in.; 47 × 59.7 cm.
X.308

General Philip Sheridan
Equestrian sculpture
Gutzon Borglum (1867–1941)
1920
Bronze
18½ × 6 × 19½ in.; 47 × 15.2 × 49.5 cm.
Gift of Flora C. Montonya
1959.327

Battle Flag of the 6th Virginia Cavalry
c. 1862
Silk
48¼ × 52 in.; 122.6 × 132.1 cm.
Charles F. Gunther Collection
1920.1633

Guidon of the Palmetto Battle Light Artillery
c. 1862
Wool, cotton
38½ × 26¼ in.; 97.8 × 66.7 cm.
Charles F. Gunther Collection
1920.1680

U.S. Sanitary Commission
Photograph
Publisher: Taylor & Huntington, Hartford,
    Connecticut
c. 1863
Albumen print
9 × 11 in.; 22.9 × 27.9 cm.
ICHi-22218

Surgeons 3rd Division 9th Corps
Photograph
Publisher: Taylor & Huntington, Hartford,
    Connecticut
c. 1864
Albumen print
9 × 11 in.; 22.9 × 27.9 cm.
ICHi-22080

Surgical Kit
Geo. Tiemann, New York
c. 1861
Instruments: steel, wooden handles
Case: wood, plush, brass fittings
Instruments vary in length from 12¾ to 6¼ in.;
    32.4 to 15.9 cm.
Case: 3 × 14 × 4⅜ in.; 7.6 × 35.6 × 11.1
    cm.
Gift of Leslie L. Cooke

Interior of an Army Hospital, 1864
Photograph
Publisher: Taylor & Huntington, Hartford,
    Connecticut
1864
Albumen print
9 × 11 in.; 22.9 × 27.9 cm.
ICHi-22081

Tent Hospital in the Field
Photograph
Haas & Peale, Morris Island and Hilton Head,
    South Carolina
1863
Albumen print
6 × 8⅝ in.; 15.2 × 21.9 cm.
ICHi-22082

"Report of Killed and Wounded"
Manuscript
Dr. David J. Griffiths
1862
Ink on paper
13⅞ × 8½ in.; 35.2 × 21.6 cm.

Medical Case (used by Surgeon E. C. Bidwell,
    U.S. Army)
1862
Case: leather, wood, plush, paper, metal, brass
Vials: glass, cork, paper
Case: 6 × 11¼ × 5 in.; 15.2 × 28.6 × 12.7
    cm.
Vials vary in length from 4¼ to 2⅛ in.; 10.8 ×
    5.4 cm.

Medical Supplies
1861–1865
a) Cotton
b,c) Canvas, wood, metal
d) Metal canister, plaster
a) 3 × 1⅜ in.; 7.6 × 3.5 cm.
b,c) 1⅞ × 2 in.; 4.8 × 5.1 cm. and 5¼ × 1½
    in.; 13.3 × 3.8 cm.
d) 7⅞ × 1⅞ in.; 20 × 4.8 cm.

Tourniquets
D. Tiemann & Co.
c. 1863
Cotton, wood, metal
5 × 2 × 2¼ in.; 12.7 × 5.1 × 5.7 cm.
1¾ × 1⅝ × 2 in.; 4.4 × 4.1 ×
    5.1 cm.

Libby Prison, Richmond, Virginia
Photograph
Rees, Richmond, Virginia
c. 1863
Albumen print
15 × 18⅛ in.; 38.1 × 46 cm.
ICHi-22083

Bricks from Libby Prison, Richmond, Virginia
c. 1850
Charles F. Gunther Collection

Diary (kept in Libby Prison, Richmond,
    Virginia)
Manuscript
William Henry Powell
August 20–September 13, 1863
Pencil on paper
4⅛ × 3⅜ in.; 10.5 × 8.6 cm.
Gift of Mrs. M. P. Stookey

Carved Eagle (made in Libby Prison,
    Richmond, Virginia)
c. 1863
Mahogany
8 × 10 × 6½ in.; 20.3 × 25.4 ×
    16.5 cm.
Charles F. Gunther Collection
1920.1102

Pincushion (made in Libby Prison, Richmond, Virginia)
Colonel William H. Powell
1863
Bone, velvet
2⅜ × 1⅜ × ⅞ in.; 6 × 3.5 × 2.2 cm.
Gift of Harry L. Powell and Mrs. Charles L. Allen
1922.42

Napkin Ring (made in Libby Prison, Richmond, Virginia)
Colonel William H. Powell
1863
Bone
1⅜ × 1 in.; 3.5 × 2.5 cm.
Gift of Harry L. Powell and Mrs. Charles L. Allen
1922.43

Napkin Ring (made in Libby Prison, Richmond, Virginia)
Colonel William H. Powell
1863
Bone
1⅜ × 1 in.; 3.5 × 2.5 cm.
Gift of Harry L. Powell and Mrs. Charles L. Allen
1922.44

Knife (made in Libby Prison, Richmond, Virginia)
Colonel William H. Powell
1863
Bone
3½ × ⅜ in.; 8.9 × 1 cm.
Gift of Harry L. Powell and Mrs. Charles L. Allen
1922.45

Cross (made in Libby Prison, Richmond, Virginia)
Colonel William H. Powell
1863
Bone, gold
1½ × ⅞ × ⅛ in.; 3.8 × 2.2 × 0.3 cm.
Gift of Harry L. Powell and Mrs. Charles L. Allen
1922.65

Pipe Head (made in Libby Prison, Richmond, Virginia)
J. L. Ligon, Jr.
c. 1863
Wood
2 × 1¼ × 2¼ in.; 5.1 × 3.2 × 5.7 cm.

Pipe Head (made in Libby Prison, Richmond, Virginia)
c. 1863
Wood
3 × 1⅝ × 2⅞ in.; 7.6 × 4.1 × 7.3 cm.
XA-219

Poker Chips (used by U.S. Army officers in Libby Prison, Richmond, Virginia)
c. 1863
Bone chips, tin container
Chip diameter: 1½ in.; 3.8 cm.
Container: 3 × 1¾ in.; 7.6 × 4.4 cm.
Charles F. Gunther Collection
1920.1108

Memento (made in Andersonville Prison, Georgia)
J. C. Farr
c. 1864
Paint on bone
1⅞ × 1¼ × ⅛ in.; 4.8 × 3.2 × 0.3 cm.
1932.232

Chain (made in Libby Prison, Richmond, Virginia)
c. 1863
Wood
Length: 140½ in.; 356.9 cm.
Charles F. Gunther Collection
1920.981

Book (made in Libby Prison, Richmond, Virginia)
c. 1863
Pine, metal
3½ × 2⅜ × 1⅜ in.; 8.9 × 6 × 3.5 cm.
Charles F. Gunther Collection
1920.1101

Spoons (used in Libby Prison, Richmond, Virginia)
c. 1863
Wood
a) 6½ × 1½ in.; 16.5 × 3.8 cm.
b) 7⅝ × 1¼ in.; 19.4 × 3.2 cm.
Charles F. Gunther Collection

Prisoners at Camp Douglas, Chicago
Photograph
1864
Albumen print
8 × 10 in.; 20.3 × 25.4 cm.
ICHi-22084

Camp Douglas, Chicago, 1862–1865
Painting
Albert E. Myers
1864
Oil on canvas mounted on board
16¾ × 22⅛ in.; 42.5 × 56.2 cm. (unframed)
Gift of George S. Hamilton
1918.5

"Twas a Pleasant Home of Ours Sister"
Sheet music
Joseph M. Dunavan, Confederate prisoner at Camp Douglas, Chicago
c. 1864
Ink and pencil on paper
8 × 10 in.; 20.3 × 25.4 cm.

"Roll of Prisoners of War Paroled at Camp Douglas"
Manuscript
November 30, 1864
Ink on paper
15⅞ × 30½ in.; 40.3 × 52.1 cm.
Gift of John T. Dale

Soldiers at Camp Douglas
Photograph
1864
Albumen print
12 × 15 in.; 30.5 × 38.1 cm.
Gift of the *Chicago Daily News*
ICHi-22085

Reading the War Bulletins in Broadway, New York
Wood engraving
Harper's Weekly
July 20, 1861
Paper
6¼ × 10¼ in.; 15.9 × 26 cm.

Chicago Tribune
Newspaper
July 4, 1863
Ink on paper
28⅜ × 21¾ in.; 72.1 × 55.2 cm.

The Press in the Field
Wood engraving
Thomas Nast
Harper's Weekly
April 30, 1864
Ink on paper
15⅝ × 21⅝ in.; 39.8 × 54.9 cm.
Gift of R. T. Anderson
ICHi-22086

Picket Guard, with George Barnard (Photographer) Sitting in Front of His Darkroom Tent
Photograph
George Barnard
c. 1863
Albumen print
14 × 17⅞ in.; 35.6 × 45.4 cm.
ICHi-09464, 07819

Walker the Artist at Work on Lookout Mountain
Photograph
Albumen print
6⅞ × 9⅞ in.; 17.5 × 25.1 cm.
ICHi-07935

Six *WAR, POLITICS, AND SOCIETY*

Abraham Lincoln
Photograph
Anthony Berger
1864
Albumen print
8½ × 6½ in.; 21.6 × 16.5 cm.
ICHi-22089

Mary Todd Lincoln
Carte de visite
Matthew B. Brady
1862
Albumen print
4 × 2½ in.; 10.2 × 6.4 cm.
Gift of Burton Holmes
ICHi-22199

Robert Todd Lincoln
Carte de visite
Matthew B. Brady
c. 1861
Albumen print
4 × 2⅝ in.; 10.2 × 6.7 cm.
Gift of John D. Searle
ICHi-22200

Thomas Lincoln
Carte de visite
Matthew B. Brady
1865
Albumen print
4 × 2½ in.; 10.2 × 6.4 cm.
ICHi-22201

William Wallace Lincoln
Carte de visite
Matthew B. Brady
c. 1861
Albumen print
4 × 2⅜ in.; 10.2 × 6 cm.
ICHi-22202

Spectacles (allegedly used by Abraham Lincoln)
c. 1863
Glass, silver
Gift of Marshall Field III
1952.75

Watch (presented to Abraham Lincoln by the
Illinois State Journal, Springfield, when he
left for Washington, D.C.)
c. 1861
Diameter: 2⅛ in.; 5.4 cm.
Gift of Frank G. Logan
1917.7

The Council of War
Sculpture
John Rogers (1829–1904)
1867
Paint on plaster
24 × 17 × 17 in.; 61 × 43.2 ×
43.2 cm.
Charles F. Gunther Collection
1920.149

Life Mask of Abraham Lincoln
Clark Mills (1810–1883)
1865
Plaster
7 × 8 × 10 in.; 17.8 × 20.3 ×
23.4 cm.
Gift of Mrs. Ellie Weir
1976.66

Letter from Abraham Lincoln to the Secretaries
of War and Navy Requesting the Testing of a
New Incendiary Shell
Manuscript
Abraham Lincoln
February 16, 1863
Ink on paper
9⅞ × 7½ in.; 25.1 × 19.1 cm.

Letter from Abraham Lincoln to
I. N. Arnold Discussing Union Army Officers
Manuscript
Abraham Lincoln
May 26, 1863
Ink on paper
9¾ × 8⅞ in.; 24.8 × 22.5 cm.

President Lincoln on Antietam Battlefield
Photograph
Alexander Gardner
October 3, 1862
Albumen print
6⅝ × 9¼ in.; 16.8 × 23.5 cm.
ICHi-11179

*President Lincoln with General McClellan at
Antietam, Md.*
Photograph
Alexander Gardner
October 3, 1862
Albumen print
9 × 7 in.; 22.9 × 17.8 cm.
ICHi-11178

$100 Reward
Broadside
H. Polkinhorn's Steam Job Printing Office,
Washington, D.C.
September 17, 1861
Ink on paper
12 × 9¼ in.; 30.5 × 23.5 cm.
ICHi-22090

*"John Henry" Contraband at Headquarters, Army
of Potomac*
Photograph
c. 1862
Albumen print
9 × 11 in.; 22.9 × 27.9 cm.
ICHi-22091

Contrabands
Carte de visite
George Barnard and James F. Gibson
1862
Albumen print
2⅝ × 4¼ in.; 6.7 × 10.8 cm.
ICHi-22092

Douglass' Monthly
Periodical
Editor: Frederick Douglass, Rochester, New
York
July 1861
Ink on paper
12⅞ × 8½ in.; 32.7 × 21.6 cm.

Correspondence Between Lizzie Little and
George Avery Concerning the Emancipation
Proclamation
Manuscript
Lizzie Little, George Avery
1862
Ink on paper
8 × 5 in.; 20.3 × 12.7 cm.
7¾ × 5⅛ in.; 19.7 × 13 cm.
Gift of Mrs. M. A. Buchanan

"Emancipation Memorial: Report of the
Delegation to President Lincoln"
Manuscript
September 1862
Ink on paper
10¼ × 8⅝ in.; 26 × 21.9 cm.

Table Upon which Abraham Lincoln Drafted
the Emancipation Proclamation
c. 1850
Mahogany
31 × 40½ × 40½ in.; 78.7 × 102.9 × 102.9
cm.
Gift of Ellen N. LaMotte
1943.72

Side Chairs (used by Abraham Lincoln and
members of his cabinet in the White House)
Attributed to J. & J. W. Meeks, New York
1846
Oak, horsehair upholstery
35⅝ × 19 × 16 in.; 90.5 × 48.3 × 40.6 cm.
Gift of Ellen N. LaMotte
1943.73ab

Emancipation Proclamation
Broadside
1863
Ink on paper
13⅛ × 8⅜ in.; 33.3 × 21.3 cm.
The Lincoln Collection
ICHi-22093

Abe Lincoln's Last Card
Wood engraving cartoon
John Tenniel
Punch
October 1862
Ink on paper
6⅞ × 8½ in.; 17.5 × 21.6 cm.
ICHi-22094

*Les nègres affranchis colportant le décret
d'affranchissement du président Lincoln* (Freed
negroes celebrating President Lincoln's decree
of emancipation)
Wood engraving
Le Monde Illustré
March 21, 1863
Ink on paper
11¾ × 15½ in.; 29.8 × 39.4 cm.
1956.413
ICHi-22095

*Programme of Arrangements and Order of
Exercises for the Inauguration of the National
Cemetery of Gettysburg, on the 19th of November,
1863*
Broadside
Gideon & Pearson, Washington, D.C.
1863
Ink on paper
8½ × 5½ in.; 21.6 × 14 cm.
Gift of Edgar J. Uihlein
ICHi-22096

*Address of Hon. Edward Everett, at the
Consecration of the National Cemetery at
Gettysburg, 19th November, 1863, with the
Dedicatory Speech of President Lincoln*
Pamphlet
Publisher: Little, Brown and Company, Boston
1864
Ink on paper
8⅝ × 11⅜ in.; 21.9 × 28.9 cm.

*Corruption and Frauds of Lincoln's
Administration*
Pamphlet
1864
Ink on paper
8⅝ × 5⅞ in.; 21.9 × 14.9 cm.

*General Burnside's Order No. 84, Suppressing the
Chicago Times, and Its History*
Pamphlet
W. F. Storey
c. 1864
Ink on paper
8½ × 5⅛ in.; 21.6 × 13 cm.

The Chicago Times
Newspaper
Publishers: W. F. Storey and A. Worden
June 9, 1863
Ink on paper
28¼ × 20¾ in.; 71.7 × 52.7 cm.

The Knight of the Rueful Countenance
Wood engraving cartoon
Adalbert J. Volck
c. 1863
Ink on paper
9⅞ × 6 in.; 25.1 × 15.2 cm.
ICHi-22097

*The Riots in New York: The Mob Lynching a
Negro in Clarkson Street*
Wood engraving
Illustrated London News
August 8, 1863
Ink on paper
7 × 11 in.; 17.8 × 27.9 cm.

*Report of the Committee of Merchants for the Relief
of Colored People Suffering from the Late Riots in
the City of New York*
Pamphlet
Publisher: George A. Whitehorne
1863
Ink on paper
8⅝ × 9½ in.; 21.9 × 24.1 cm.
Gift of Samuel S. Otis

Élections presidentielles en Amérique (Presidential
elections in America)
Wood engraving
Le Monde Illustré
1864
Ink on paper
10¼ × 14½ in.; 26.0 × 36.8 cm.
1956.412

*The Watervliet United States Arsenal at Troy, New
York*
Wood engravings
Frank Leslie's Illustrated Newspaper
August 17, 1861
Ink on paper
15¾ × 22 in.; 40 × 55.9 cm.

*Filling Cartridges at the United States Arsenal of
Watertown, Massachusetts*
Wood engraving
Winslow Homer
Harper's Weekly
July 20, 1861
Ink on paper
12⅛ × 10½ in.; 30.8 × 26.7 cm.

*Manufacturing Muskets, U.S. Armory, Springfield,
Mass.*
Wood engraving
Harper's Weekly
September 21, 1861
Ink on paper
15¾ × 10½ in.; 40 × 26.7 cm.

.52 Caliber Breech Loading Carbine
Massachusetts Arms Company, Chicopee Falls,
Massachusetts
c. 1863
Walnut, steel, brass
Length: 39½ in.; 100.3 cm.
Charles F. Gunther Collection
1920.75

.44 Caliber Percussion Revolver
Remington Arms Company, Ilion, New York
Patented 1861
Wood, steel
13¾ × 5 in.; 34.9 × 12.7 cm.
Gift of Charles H. Walgreen, Jr.
1969.623

*Cartridge Box (from the Watervliet United States
Arsenal, Troy, New York)*
c. 1863
Wood
6¾ × 9 × 20 in.; 17.1 × 22.9 ×
50.8 cm.
1976.74.30

Cartridges and Wrapper
Hazard Powder Co.
Patented 1862
Metal, paper
1½ × 3⅛ × ⅝ in.; 3.8 × 7.9 ×
1.6 cm.
1976.74.38

Cartridges and Wrapper
Johnston & Dow, New York
Patented 1861, 1862
Metal, paper
1⅞ × 3 × ⅜ in.; 4.8 × 7.6 × 1 cm.
1976.74.39

Letters with Bids for Manufacturing Uniforms
Manuscripts
A. J. Lane & Co., Philadelphia
Whiting, Galloupe, Bliss and Co., Boston
Rockhill & Wilson, Philadelphia
May 1861
Ink on paper; wool fabric samples

U.S. Army Artillery Jacket
Private of light artillery
1861–1865
Wool
22½ × 17 in.; 57.6 × 43.2 cm.
Sleeve length: 24¼ in.; 62.2 cm.
XA-1851

*Members of the Soldiers Aid Society, Springfield,
Illinois*
Photograph
c. 1863
Albumen print
7⅞ × 10 in.; 20 × 25.4 cm.
Gift of Mrs. L. J. Tilton
ICHi-22103

To the Loyal Women of America
Broadside
1861
Ink on paper
19⅞ × 12½ in.; 50.5 × 31.8 cm.
Gift of J. R. Getz
ICHi-22100

Heroes & Heroines of the War
Color wood engraving
c. 1863
Thomas Nast
Publisher: Ensign & Bridgman, New York
Ink on paper
10 × 13⅞ in.; 25.4 × 35.2 cm.
Gift of Dr. Otto L. Schmidt
ICHi-22101

Doll and Trunk of Clothes (purchased at the
    Northwestern Sanitary Fair, Chicago)
Dressed by the Dunham Family of Chicago and
    donated to the Fair
1865
Doll: wax over composition, silk, wool, cotton
Trunk: wood covered with paper
Doll height: 21½ in.; 54.6 cm.
Trunk: 6⅞ × 12½ × 7½ in.; 17.5 × 31.8 ×
    19.1 cm.
Gift of Miss Mary B. Dunham
1924.30

Tickets to the Northwestern Sanitary Fair,
    Chicago
a) 1863
b) 1865
Ink on paper
a) 1½ × 2¾ in.; 3.8 × 7 cm.
b) 2⅜ × 3½ in.; 5.9 × 8.9 cm.

*Main Building of the Great Northwestern Sanitary
    Fair, Chicago*
Color lithograph
Baker & Company
1865
Ink on Paper
16 × 21⅝ in.; 40.6 × 54.9 cm.
Gift of George H. Laflin
ICHi-22142

Dueling Pistols (purchased at the Northwestern
    Sanitary Fair, Chicago)
Plant's Manufacturing Co.
Merwin & Bray, New York
1865
Pistols: rosewood, steel, silver-washed mounts
Box: walnut, brass, velvet lining
Pistol: 4½ × 10 in.; 11.4 × 25.4 cm.
Box: 2¼ × 8½ × 8½ in.; 5.7 × 21.6 × 21.6
    cm.
Gift of Mrs. H. H. Reuss, Mrs. Julian S. Mason,
    and Mr. Walter C. Grey

Potholders (sold at the Northwestern Sanitary
    Fair, Chicago; with mottoes: "Any Holder but
    a Slaveholder" and "We's Free")
c. 1865
a) Cotton, felt, yarn
b) Burlap, felt, yarn
a) 7 × 7 in.; 17.8 × 17.8 cm.
b) 8¼ × 5¾ in.; 21 × 14.6 cm.
b) Gift of Mrs. Hugh C. Crowgy and Mrs. W.
    A. O'Bannon, Jr.
b) 1969.1737

Ribbons of the Executive Committee,
    Northwestern Sanitary Fair, Chicago
c. 1865
Silk
a) 8⅝ × 4⅛ in.; 21.9 × 10.5 cm.
b) 11 × 3 in.; 27.9 × 7.6 cm.

Diorama Depicting Black and White Children
    Playing Together (purchased at the
    Northwestern Sanitary Fair, Chicago)
1865
Case: wood
Figures: wax, cloth
15⅜ × 18¾ × 12 in.; 39.1 × 47.6 × 30.5 cm.
Gift of Miss Marie S. Gale
1953.358

N.W. Sanitary Commission & Soldiers' Home Fair
Broadside
1865
Ink on paper
9¾ × 7⅝ in.; 24.8 × 19.4 cm.
Gift of Mrs. Carroll Paul
ICHi-20293

Mary A. Livermore
Cabinet card
Veeder, Albany, New York
c. 1880
Albumen print
6½ × 4¼ in.; 16.5 × 10.8 cm.
Gift of Gerald Grant
ICHi-22144

The Agitator
Periodical
Editor: Mary A. Livermore, Chicago
May 22, 1869
Ink on paper
17 × 12¼ in.; 43.2 × 31.1 cm.

My Story of the War
Book
Mary A. Livermore
Publisher: A. D. Worthington and Co.,
    Hartford, Connecticut
1888
Ink on paper
9⅛ × 6⅛ × 2¼ in.; 23.2 × 15.6 × 5.7 cm.
    (closed)
9⅛ × 11¾ × 2 in.; 23.2 × 29.8 ×
    5.1 cm. (open)

*Sowing and Reaping: Richmond Women's Bread
    Riot*
Wood engraving
Frank Leslie's Illustrated Newspaper
May 23, 1863
Ink on paper
7 × 10¼ in.; 17.8 × 26 cm.

The Daily Citizen
Newspaper
Editor: J. M. Swords, Vicksburg, Mississippi
a) June 27, 1863
b) June 30, 1863
a) Ink on wallpaper
b) Ink on wallpaper
a) 19⅞ × 12 in.; 50.5 × 30.5 cm.
b) 16½ × 12¼ in.; 42 × 31.1 cm.

"Order for Impressment of Stock"
Manuscript
H. W. Feilden
December 30, 1864
Ink on paper
6½ × 8 in.; 16.5 × 20.3 cm.
Charles F. Gunther Collection

City of Atlanta, Georgia, No. 2
Rebel Works in Front of Atlanta, Georgia, No. 1
The Potter House, Atlanta
*Ruins of the R.R. Depot, Charleston, South
    Carolina*
Columbia from the Capitol
Destruction of Hood's Ordinance Train
Photographs
George Barnard
1864–1865
Albumen prints
15½ × 9 in.; 39.4 × 22.9 cm.
ICHi-22105–22110

"Description of Sherman's Campaign"
Manuscript
J. R. Zearing
December 15, 1864
Ink on paper
13¼ × 8¼ in.; 33.7 × 21 cm.
Gift of Mrs. Kingsley Colton

General W. T. Sherman and Staff
Photograph
Publisher: Taylor & Huntington, Hartford,
    Connecticut
1864
Albumen print
9 × 11 in.; 22.9 × 27.9 cm.
ICHi-22147

Confederate Railroad Track Bent by Union
    Forces
1864–1865
Iron
5¼ × 82 × 11½ in.; 13.3 × 208.3 × 29.2 cm.
Charles F. Gunther Collection

"Map of the Plot of Vicksburg and Natchez
    Districts for the Leasing of Abandoned
    Plantations"
Map
Middleton, Strobridge and Co.
c. 1863
Ink on paper
67 × 18½ in.; 170.2 × 47 cm.

Letter from Robert E. Lee to Secretary of War,
    John C. Breckenridge, Advising Him to Leave
    Richmond
Manuscript
Robert E. Lee
March 7, 1865
Ink on paper
9¾ × 8 in.; 24.8 × 20.3 cm.
Charles F. Gunther Collection

The Evacuation of Richmond, Virginia
Color lithograph
Currier & Ives, New York
1865
Ink on paper
13½ × 17¾ in.; 34.3 × 45.1 cm.
ICHi-22114

Ruins of Richmond
Photographs
Alexander Gardner
1865
Albumen prints
a) 9¼ × 10¾ in.; 23.5 × 27.3 cm.
b) 7⅜ × 10⅛ in.; 18.7 × 25.7 cm.
a) ICHi-22115
b) ICHi-22116

Freedmen at Richmond
Photograph
L. C. Handy Studios, Washington, D.C.
1865
Copy print from original albumen print
5 × 8¼ in.; 12.7 × 21 cm.
ICHi-22117

Glory! Richmond and Petersburg Ours!!
Broadside
Jamestown Journal
April 3, 1865
Ink on paper
13 × 6⅝ in.; 33 × 16.8 cm.
ICHi-22118

Lincoln's Drive Through Richmond
Painting
Dennis Malone Carter (1820–1881)
1866
Oil on canvas
45 × 68 in.; 114.3 × 172.7 cm.
Gift of Mr. Philip K. Wrigley
1955.398

"The Heading off of Lee's Army"
Newspaper article
New York Herald
April 7, 1865
Ink on paper
22¾ × 16⅛ in.; 57.8 × 41 cm.

Letter from Abraham Lincoln to General Ulysses
    S. Grant: "Let the thing be pressed."
Manuscript
Abraham Lincoln
April 7, 1865
Ink on paper
9⅞ × 4 in.; 25.1 × 22.2 cm.
Charles F. Gunther Collection

The Lost Cause—Lee Waiting for Grant
Painting
Thomas Nast (1840–1902)
c. 1870
Oil on canvas
69⅜ × 49⅝ in.; 176.2 × 126 cm.
Gift of Mr. Sterling Morton
1956.99

Table Upon which Robert E. Lee Signed Terms
    of Surrender, McClean Home, Appomattox
    Court House, Virginia
c. 1850
Mahogany veneers over pine, mahogany, marble
30¾ × 35½ × 35½ in.; 78.1 × 90.2 × 90.2
    cm.
Charles F. Gunther Collection
1920.750

Telegraph Key and Receiver Used to Relay the
    News of Surrender, Railroad Depot,
    Appomattox Court House, Virginia
James J. Clark, Philadelphia
c. 1860
Brass, copper, wood, iron
Receiver: 4 × 11⅜ × 4⅞ in.; 10.2 × 28.9 ×
    12.4 cm.
Key: 6 × 5 × 1¼ in.; 15.2 × 12.7 × 3.2 cm.
Charles F. Gunther Collection
1920.905ab

Extra Dispatch. Lee's Surrender!
Broadside
1865
Ink on paper
14 × 6⅝ in.; 35.6 × 16.8 cm.
Gift of R. D. Stuart
ICHi-22119

General Lee's Farewell Address
Broadside
Johnson & Schaffter, Lynchburg, Virginia
April 10, 1865
Ink on paper
7¼ × 4¾ in.; 18.4 × 12.1 cm.
ICHi-22120

John Wilkes Booth
Cabinet card
D. W. Wilson, Hartford, Connecticut
c. 1860
Albumen prints
4¼ × 2⅜ in.; 11.4 × 6 cm.
ICHi-22212

The Assassination of President Lincoln
Color lithograph
Currier & Ives, New York
1865
Ink on paper
11¾ × 16¼ in.; 29.8 × 41.3 cm.
1935.46
ICHi-22121

Bed Upon which Abraham Lincoln Died (from
    the Peterson home, Washington, D.C.)
c. 1850
Walnut
Headboard: 46⅛ × 53¾ in.; 117.2 × 136.5 cm.
Footboard: 44½ × 53¾ in.; 113 × 136.5 cm.
Length: 78½ in.; 199.4 cm.
Charles F. Gunther Collection
1920.249ab

Bureau (from the Peterson home, Washington,
    D.C.)
c. 1850
Walnut
39½ × 43½ × 19¼ in.; 100.3 × 110.5 × 48.9
    cm.
Charles F. Gunther Collection
1920.250

Rocking Chair (from the Peterson home,
    Washington, D.C.)
c. 1850
Painted wood
40¾ × 21 × 18½ in.; 103.5 × 53.3 × 47 cm.
Charles F. Gunther Collection
1920.251

Gas Jet (from the Peterson home, Washington,
    D.C.)
c. 1860
Brass
16 × 11 in.; 40.6 × 27.9 cm.
Charles F. Gunther Collection
1920.252

Candlestick (from the Peterson home,
    Washington, D.C.)
c. 1860
Pewter
4 × 6 in.; 10.2 × 15.2 cm.
Charles F. Gunther Collection
1920.254

The Death of Lincoln
Painting
Alonzo Chappel (1828–1887)
1868
Oil on canvas
52 × 89½ in.; 132.1 × 227.3 cm.
1971.177

"Assassination of Lincoln"
Newspaper article
New York Herald
April 15, 1865
Ink on paper
22½ × 16¼ in.; 57.2 × 41.3 cm.

Mourning Banner for Abraham Lincoln—"We
    Mourn the Great & Good"
1865
Ink on cambric
8¼ × 10⅝ in.; 21 × 27 cm.
Gift of Dr. Otto L. Schmidt
1934.170a

Mourning Banner for Abraham Lincoln—"With
    Malice Toward None with Charity for All"
1865
Ink on cambric
15⅛ × 18 in.; 38.4 × 45.7 cm.
Gift of Dr. Otto L. Schmidt
1934.169c

*Funeral Procession for Abraham Lincoln in
    Chicago*
Photograph
1865
Copy print from original albumen print
8 × 10 in.; 20.3 × 25.4 cm.
ICHi-22122

Order of Procession for Lincoln Funeral in Chicago
Broadside
1865
Ink on paper
12 × 9 in.; 30.5 × 22.9 cm.
ICHi-22123

Funeral Regalia Worn by John Jones at the
    Lincoln Funeral Procession in Chicago
1865
Crepe, silk
30¾ × 12 in.; 78.1 × 30.5 cm.
Gift of Mrs. L. Jones Lee
1905.5

Maker's Plate from Lincoln's Funeral Train
U.S. Military Railroad Car Shop
1864
Brass
4⅛ × 5¼ × ¼ in.; 10.5 × 13.3 ×
    0.6 cm.
Charles F. Gunther Collection
1920.220

"National Funeral March Dedicated to the Loyal
    Hearts of America"
Sheet music
J. E. Schonacker
Publisher: John Church, Cincinnati, Ohio
1865
Ink on paper
14 × 10¾ in.; 35.6 × 27.3 cm.

*Time Table for the Special Train, Conveying the
    Funeral Cortege with the Remains of the Late
    President from Chicago to Springfield*
Broadside
Chicago & Alton Railroad Company
1865
Ink on paper
8 × 12 in.; 20.3 × 30.5 cm.

Bracelet (allegedly used by Mary Todd Lincoln
    as mourning jewelry)
c. 1865
Charles F. Gunther Collection
1920.915

Brooch (allegedly used by Mary Todd Lincoln
    as mourning jewelry)
c. 1865
Onyx, gold
Gift of John R. Thompson, Jr.
1952.78

Brooch (allegedly used by Mary Todd Lincoln
    as mourning jewelry)
c. 1865
Gold, enamel
Gift of John R. Thompson, Jr.
1952.80

Earring (allegedly used by Mary Todd Lincoln
    as mourning jewelry)
c. 1865
Onyx
Gift of John R. Thompson, Jr.
1952.79

Mourning fan (allegedly used by Mary Todd
    Lincoln)
c. 1865
Chiffon
Length: 13¾ in.; 34.9 cm.
Gift of Dr. Frank W. Gunsaulus
1917.26

Eagle Figure (from the head of Lincoln's funeral
    bier in Chicago)
1865
Marble
16 × 30½ × 14 in.; 40.6 × 77.5 × 35.6 cm.
Gift of Mrs. L. L. Loehr
1937.30

Leaves of Grass
Book
Walt Whitman
Publisher: Rees Welsh & Co., Philadelphia
1882
Ink on paper
7⅝ × 5⅜ × 1¼ in.; 19.3 × 13.6 × 3.2 cm.
    (closed)

Lincoln Mourning Badges
1865
Silk, paper, tin
a) 4¾ × 5¾ in.; 12.1 × 14.6 cm.
b) 5¼ × 3 in.; 13.3 × 7.6 cm.
a) Gift of Caroline D. Wade

Lincoln Mourning Ribbon
T. Stevens, Coventry, England
1865
Machine-embroidered silk
9⅝ × 2⅛ in.; 24.4 × 5.4 cm.

Funeral Vases (used in the Chicago funeral
    services for Abraham Lincoln)
c. 1865
Porcelain
Height: 13¼ in.; 33.7 cm.
Gift of Augustus H. Burley
1917.14ab

*Grand Review of the Great Veteran Armies of
    Grant & Sherman at Washington on the 23rd
    and 24th May, 1865*
Stereograph
Brady & Co., Washington, D.C.
Publisher: E. & H. T. Anthony, New York
Albumen print
3⅜ × 7 in.; 8.6 × 17.8 cm.
Gift of Mrs. J. Rockefeller Prentice

EPILOGUE *THE WAR'S AFTERMATH*

The First Vote
Wood engraving
Alfred R. Waud
Harper's Weekly
November 16, 1867
Ink on paper
16 × 10⅞ in.; 40.6 × 27.6 cm.

The Fifteenth Amendment
Color lithograph
Th. Kelly, New York
1870
Ink on paper
11⅛ × 14 in.; 28. 3 × 35.6 cm.
ICHi-22124

Ceremonial Copy of the Thirteenth Amendment,
   signed by Abraham Lincoln, Hannibal
   Hamlin, Schuyler Colfax, and members of the
   U.S. Senate and House of Representatives
Manuscript
February 1, 1865
Ink on paper
21 × 14½ in.; 53.34 × 36.83 cm.
Charles F. Gunther Collection

The Shackle Broken by the Genius of Freedom
Color lithograph
E. Sachs & Co., Baltimore
1874
Ink on paper
21½ × 26½ in.; 54.6 × 67.3 cm.
ICHi-22125

*Two Members of the Ku-Klux Klan in Their
   Disguises*
Wood engraving
Harper's Weekly
December 19, 1868
Ink on paper
9 × 7 in.; 22.9 × 17.8 cm.

The Lost Cause
Lithograph
Currier & Ives, New York
1871
Ink on paper
11⅞ × 16 in.; 30.2 × 40.6 cm.
ICHi-22126

William Henry Lamb Wallace Commemorative
   Photograph
Photograph
W. E. Bowman, Ottawa, Illinois
1884
Albumen print
12 × 10 in.; 30.5 × 25.4 cm.
Gift of F. S. Bayden
ICHi-22153

INDEX